ANNUAL REPORT OF THE U.S.A.
FY 2012

PRESENTED BY

INSTITUTE OF POLITICS AT HARVARD UNIVERSITY

AMERICAN EDUCATION FOUNDATION

Staff

PUBLISHER
Meredith Bagby
Executive Director, American Education Foundation

EXECUTIVE EDITOR
Henry Shull

SENIOR EDITORS
Alex Palmer
Victor Yang

WRITERS
Daniel Backman
Marina Bolotnikova
Christine Hurd
Elsa Kania
John Kocsis
Sandra Korn
Alex Palmer
Divya Seth
Matt Shuham
Henry Shull
Cassandra Thomson
Andres Uribe
Rachel Wong

CREATIVE/PRODUCTION
Susan Woitovich

Published by Principio Books, LLC.
14525 SW Millikan Way, #75822
Beaverton, Oregon 97005
info@principiobooks.com
www.principiobooks.com

PRINCIPIO

ISBN: 1629080004

ISBN-13: 978-1-62908-000-0

TABLE OF CONTENTS

A Note on the Figures in this Report

Although this edition of the Annual Report of the United States of America is being released in summer 2013, it primarily covers spending figures for the federal budget for fiscal year 2012, which lasted from October 1, 2011, to September 30, 2012. The gap between the fiscal year and the issuing of this report is due to the fact that the federal budget process for a single fiscal year stretches across several calendar years: President Obama issued his budget request for FY 2012 on February 14, 2011, but Congress did not vote to approve large-scale budget legislation until fall 2011, and year-end spending reports (reflecting actual rather than approved use of funds) were not available until late 2012. Despite this primary focus on FY 2012, though, this edition of ARUSA includes some recent developments, including the effects of the American Taxpayer Relief Act of 2012, which was passed in early January 2013.

Second, in addition to the date of figures in this report, please note that throughout this report some data series are adjusted for inflation and others are not. Economists describe data that are adjusted for the natural rise of prices over time as being in "real" terms; data that are not adjusted for inflation are said to be in "nominal" terms or in "current dollars." To use a concrete example from this report—drawn from Figure 31, "Defense Spending, 1962-2012 (real)"—the U.S. government purchased all its weapons, paid all its soldiers, and covered all other defense-related expenses in 1970 for $81.7 billion. This figure is in "nominal" terms, also known as "current dollars." However, if the U.S. wanted to buy the same set of weapons, pay the same number of soldiers, and cover all of the same expenses in 2005, it would have had to pay $463.9 billion, because prices and wages rose substantially over 35 years. This larger figure is in "real" terms, also known as "2005 dollars."

Finally, note that not all figures may add to stated totals due to rounding.

★

INTRODUCTION

by The Editors

> **"A billion here, a billion there, pretty soon you're talking about real money."**
> **—Attributed to Sen. Everett M. Dirksen (1896-1969)**

American taxpayers are shareholders in the world's largest corporation.

This is the metaphor at the heart of the following report, the Annual Report of the United States of America (ARUSA).

If the U.S. were a publicly traded corporation, it would be required to issue an annual report to its shareholders at the time of its annual meeting. Most of these reports are professionally designed, with plenty of graphs and tables to describe exactly how the company got its income and spent its money in the previous year. In addition, corporations in the U.S. are required to complete a 10-K, a detailed report mandated by the Securities and Exchange Commission that includes information on the business's activities, risk factors, governance, executive compensation, and other topics, along with extensive financial data.

But the U.S. government does not issue an annual report, put on a shareholder's meeting, or complete anything like a Form 10-K. Despite the substantial annual investments of taxpayer-shareholders, there is no central source of financial information, signed by top federal executives and made publicly accessible. Instead, financial information is spread across thousands of reports on hundreds of websites for departments, agencies, bureaus, boards, commissions, enterprises, and other programs.

Given the overwhelming size and complexity of the modern U.S. federal government, it is not feasible to expect all taxpayers to have the time necessary to sort through thousands of news articles and government reports or to figure out the intricacies of the budgeting process.

ARUSA brings the experts and sources to you. Interviews with professors at America's top universities and data extracted from the most relevant documents make an overwhelming volume of information easily digestible for the busy taxpayer. Put simply, ARUSA wants to increase government accountability and transparency with respect to budgetary issues, telling you what happens with your money every year.

The budget is of greater importance now than at almost any other point in our nation's history. Indeed, budget decisions have substantial effects on national security, social strength, and American character. With respect to international relations, economic decisions at the federal level affect defense spending, trade policy, and other factors that make our country more or less exposed to international pressures. Domestically, funding for scientific research and K-12 education supports America's tradition of pioneering intellectual achievement, and allocations for Head Start and welfare programs support the development of the next generation of all citizens.

But scarcity is a problem that all governments will face. Even in times of global economic growth, leaders must make challenging decisions about how to allocate limited funds. Growth in education spending means a cut in allocations toward defense, health care, or some other initiative (or, less politically palatable, an increase in taxes).

Taken collectively, these decisions make a statement about America's priorities. What a Republican might see as incentive-crushing government hand-outs, a Democrat might see as morally required support for the less fortunate. Programs that one citizen might view as allowing free industry could be seen by another as detrimental to the environment or to consumers. As such, budgetary decisions are fundamentally political and moral, and they should not be taken lightly.

In short, the future of our country depends heavily on the budgeting choices made by decision-makers in the federal government. Knowing how taxes are allocated, understanding how those decisions were made, and having a general understanding of the government's financial position provide the necessary foundation for engagement with the government at all levels to ensure that difficult choices are intelligently made and reflect the will of the people it represents. This is vital in making sure that America will enjoy a strong, democratic future.

To this end, we present in the following pages information on the government's spending in the past year. Our report begins with articles that provide an overview of the federal government's current financial position. This section includes an income statement, which provides an overview of income and expenditures in fiscal years 2010-2014. It also includes articles on the debt and deficit, net interest, and taxes.

Later in the report, our writers offer up details on specific areas of spending, including post-recession initiatives, welfare/social safety net spending, education, and science.

We hope that this project will encourage you to engage with your representatives in government and with your fellow citizens. To start with, you can write your Senators or U.S. Representative in Washington, D.C. To promote awareness of budgetary issues, you can spread the word about ARUSA. Send your family and friends a link to our report, or share the link on Facebook or Twitter.

Also, we hope that these articles will rouse you to learn more about how the government spends your money. If a fact or statistic strikes you as surprising, use the references provided in footnotes to look up original sources and learn more about the topic.

ARUSA is a joint project of the American Education Foundation (www.americafound.org), a nonprofit organization dedicated to inspiring students of all ages to active civic engagement, and the *Harvard Political Review* (www.harvardpolitics.com), a journal of domestic and international affairs at Harvard University's Institute of Politics. If you would like to support ARUSA's mission of increasing national awareness of budgetary issues, please consider making a donation to the American Education Foundation to ensure that we can continue this work into the future.

We hope you enjoy our work, and we sincerely hope that it fulfills our mission of increasing civic knowledge, boosting awareness of budgetary issues, and spurring engagement with government and among citizens.

The Editors

AMERICA'S FINANCES: INCOME STATEMENT

TOTAL FEDERAL RECEIPTS *(In millions of dollars)*

By Type	2010	2011	2012 estimate	2013 estimate	2014 estimate	% of Total Receipts (2012)
Individual Income Tax	$898,549	$1,091,473	$1,164,650	$1,359,260	$1,476,315	47.2%
%Change		21.5%	6.7%	16.7%	8.6%	
Corporate Income Tax	$191,437	$181,085	$236,801	$347,741	$429,595	9.6%
%Change		-5.4%	30.8%	46.8%	23.5%	
Social Security & Retirement Payments	$864,814	$818,792	$840,650	$959,057	$1,038,701	34.1%
%Change		21.5%	6.7%	16.7%	8.6%	
-- On Budget	$233,127	$253,004	$268,510	$281,646	$296,262	
-- Off Budget	$631,687	$565,788	$572,140	$677,411	$742,439	
Excise Taxes	$66,909	$72,381	$79,415	$88,055	$98,575	3.2%
%Change		8.2%	9.7%	10.9%	11.9%	
Other	$141,015	$139,735	$147,083	$147,843	$172,107	6.0%
%Change		-0.9%	5.3%	0.5%	16.4%	
Total Receipts	**$2,162,724**	**$2,303,466**	**$2,468,599**	**$2,901,956**	**$3,215,293**	

TOTAL FEDERAL SPENDING *(In millions of dollars)*

By Function	2010	2011	2012 estimate	2013 estimate	2014 estimate	% of Budget (2012)
National Defense	$693,586	$705,625	$716,300	$701,767	$599,295	18.9%
%Change		1.7%	1.5%	-2.0%	-14.6%	
Social Security	$706,737	$730,811	$778,574	$825,872	$873,851	20.5%
%Change		3.4%	6.5%	6.1%	5.8%	
Income Security	622,210	597,352	579,578	559,413	539,171	15.3%
%Change		-4.0%	-3.0%	-3.5%	-3.6%	
Medicare	$451,636	$485,653	$484,486	$530,246	$558,301	12.8%
%Change		7.5%	-0.2%	9.4%	5.3%	
Health Care (includes Medicaid)	$369,054	$372,500	$361,625	$385,868	$480,269	9.5%
%Change		0.9%	-2.9%	6.7%	24.5%	
Net interest	$196,194	$229,968	$224,784	$247,715	$309,136	5.9%
%Change		17.2%	-2.3%	10.2%	24.8%	
Education, Training, Employment & Social Services	$127,710	$101,233	$139,212	$122,135	$108,675	3.7%
%Change		-20.7%	37.5%	-12.3%	-11.0%	
Veterans Benefits and Services	$108,384	$127,189	$129,605	$140,117	$146,753	3.4%
%Change		17.4%	1.9%	8.1%	4.7%	
Transportation	$91,972	$92,965	$102,552	$114,228	$107,682	2.7%
Administration of Justice	$54,385	$56,055	$62,016	$62,792	$57,291	1.6%
International Affairs	$45,195	$45,685	$56,252	$59,556	$53,749	1.5%
Natural Resources & Environment	$43,662	$45,470	$42,829	$41,312	$39,057	1.1%
General Science, Space & Technology	$30,098	$29,466	$30,991	$31,265	$30,057	0.8%
Community & Regional Development	$23,804	$23,816	$31,685	$34,983	$28,298	0.8%
General Government	$23,031	$25,507	$31,763	$26,266	$26,532	0.8%
Agriculture	$21,356	$20,661	$19,173	$25,624	$18,611	0.0%
Energy	$11,613	$12,174	$23,270	$13,914	$14,258	0.5%
Offsetting Receipts & Allowances	-$164,414	-$94,691	-$2,367	-$105,542	-$93,357	
Total, Federal Outlays	**$3,456,213**	**$3,603,061**	**$3,795,547**	**$3,803,364**	**$3,883,095**	
Total Deficit (Receipts - Spending)	**-$1,293,489**	**-$1,299,595**	**-$1,326,948**	**-$901,408**	**-$667,802**	

AMERICA'S FINANCES: FEDERAL DEFICIT AND DEBT

by Henry Shull

WHAT IS THE DEBT?

Government debt is a measure of how much money the government owes to its creditors.

In most cases, the government owes money to external creditors. For example, if the U.S. federal government signs a contract with Boeing, promising to pay $2 billion in exchange for a squadron of fighter jets, then $2 billion is added to the measure of federal debt until the U.S. government has sent Boeing payment for the jets and settled the contractual obligation. This kind of debt is known as debt held by the public.

However, the government can also owe money to itself. In the case of intra-governmental holdings, one part of the government has borrowed money from another part of the government, and the amount borrowed contributes to the overall measure of federal debt until it is repaid. For example, parts of the U.S. federal government often borrow from the Medicare or Medicaid trust funds, which currently have more money than needed for payments. However, these trust fund balances must be replenished, creating an obligation on the parts of the federal government that borrow from them.

The overall federal debt, known as total public debt outstanding, is calculated by adding together the debt held by the public and the amount of intra-governmental holdings.

In contrast to debt, the government's annual surplus or deficit is a relative measure of revenue and expenditures in a given year. If the government takes in more money through taxes than it spends in a given year, the government runs a surplus. If, however, it makes less than it spends, it runs a deficit.

Economists call measures like annual deficit or surplus a flow variable. These variables express the change in a quantity's value over time. In contrast, measures that express a quantity's value at any single point in time, like the overall federal debt, are known as stock variables.

A related concept in the United States is the federal debt limit, also known as the debt ceiling. This is a limit imposed by Congress on how much debt the federal government can incur; in other words, it is a cap on how much the government can take out in loans. The debt limit was introduced in a limited form in 1917, and it took its contemporary shape in 1939. Recently, there have been heated debates in Congress related to the debt limit, with Republicans generally arguing that the government spends too much money and that the debt limit should be kept in place. In reality, though, the debt limit has been modified over 90 times since 1940, and Congress itself authorizes the spending that creates the need to raise the debt limit.

DEFICITS, SURPLUSES, AND THE DEBT IN RECENT HISTORY

Under Bill Clinton, the U.S. began to have a yearly spending surplus rather than deficit. Largely because of the leadership of President Clinton and his Secretary of the Treasury, Robert Rubin, the federal government accrued more in receipts than in outlays from FY 1998 to FY 2001. (These were the first surpluses since 1969.) As a result, debt decreased as a percentage of GDP. At the end of FY 1991 the ratio of gross federal debt to GDP was 60.7 percent, and at the end of FY 2001 that number had dropped to 56.4 percent.

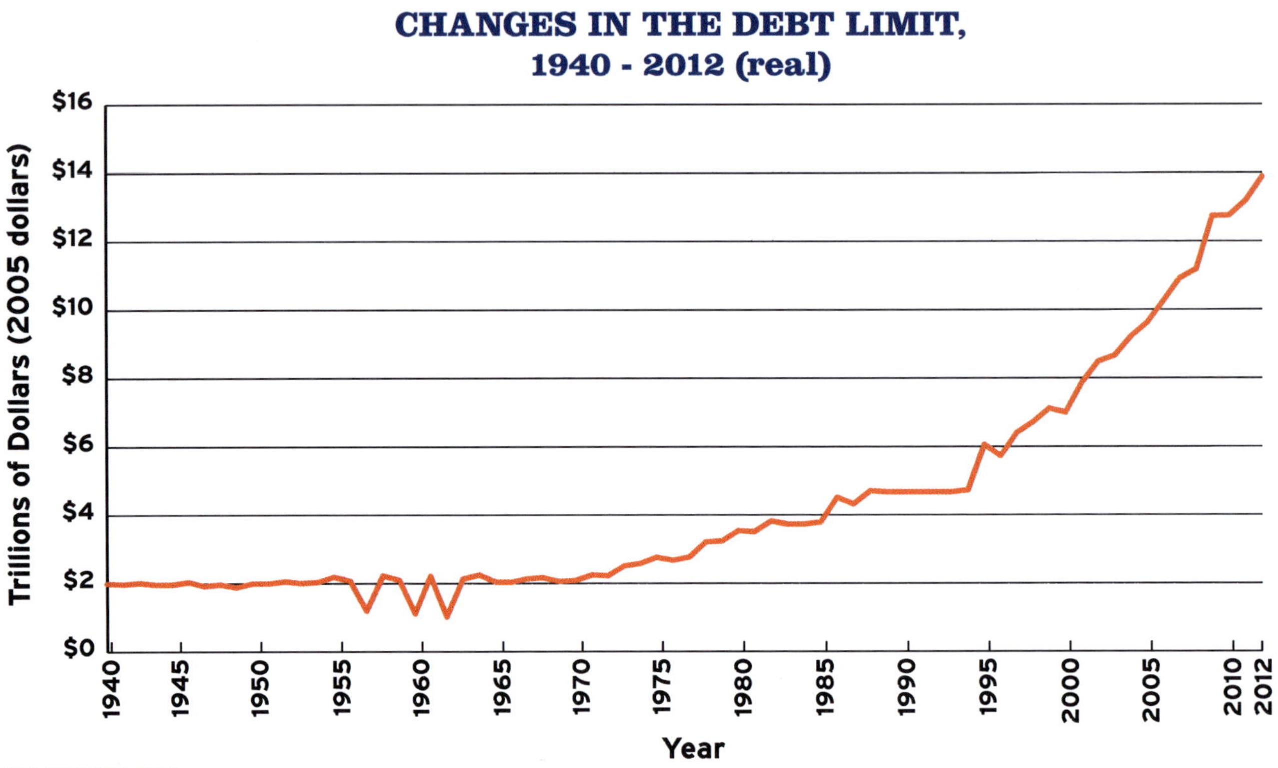

FIGURE 1 SOURCE: Budget of the U.S. Government FY 2013, http://www.gpo.gov/fdsys/pkg/BUDGET-2013-TAB/xls/BUDGET-2013-TAB-7-3.xls.

President George W. Bush's administration reversed this trend. Bush came into office with a relatively weak economy, largely a result of the dot-com bubble and the precipitous drops in economic activity following the September 11, 2001, terrorist attacks. As President, Bush decreased government revenue through a series of tax cuts, and he simultaneously increased government spending substantially through wars in Afghanistan and in Iraq and through a new Medicare prescription drug benefit plan, Part D.

At the end of the Bush administration and the beginning of the Obama administration, the government spent very large amounts of money on stimulus packages, ranging from "bailouts" of U.S. banks and automobile manufacturers to infrastructure improvements. These payments were meant to help the U.S. economy recover from the housing crisis and subsequent economic collapse that began in late 2007 and reached its nadir in late 2008.

As a consequence of all these factors, from FY 2001 to FY 2009, the gross debt-to-GDP ratio increased from 56.4 percent to 85.2 percent.

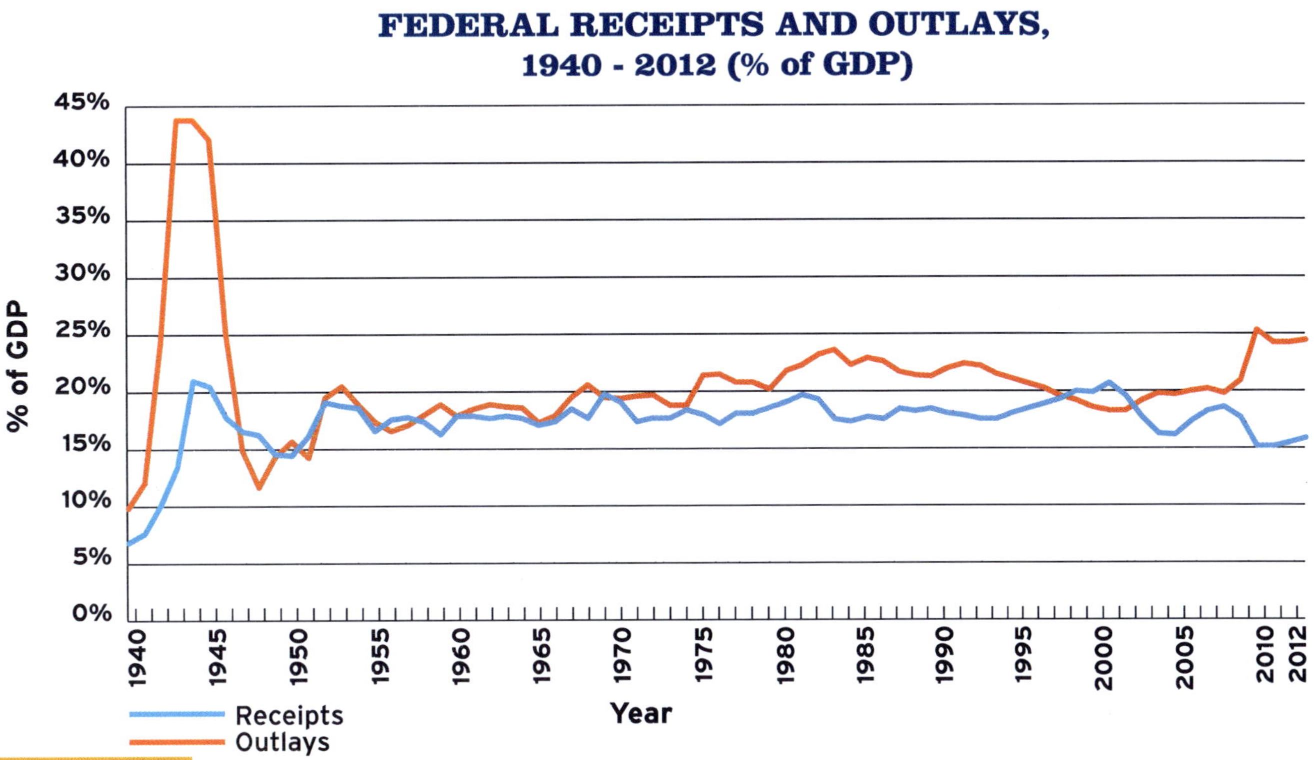

FIGURE 2

SOURCE: Budget of the U.S. Government FY 2013, http://www.gpo.gov/fdsys/pkg/BUDGET-2013-TAB/xls/BUDGET-2013-TAB-1-3.xls.

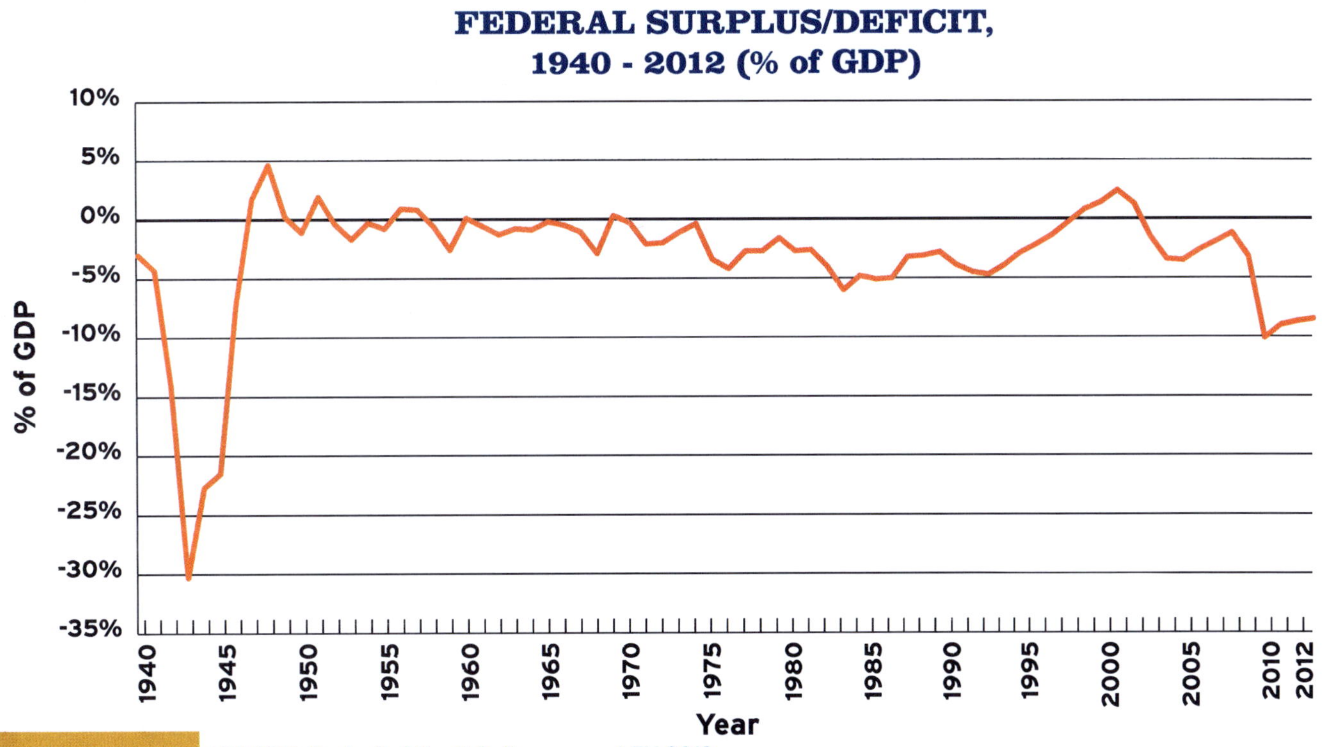

FIGURE 3

SOURCE: Budget of the U.S. Government FY 2013, http://www.gpo.gov/fdsys/pkg/BUDGET-2013-TAB/xls/BUDGET-2013-TAB-1-3.xls.

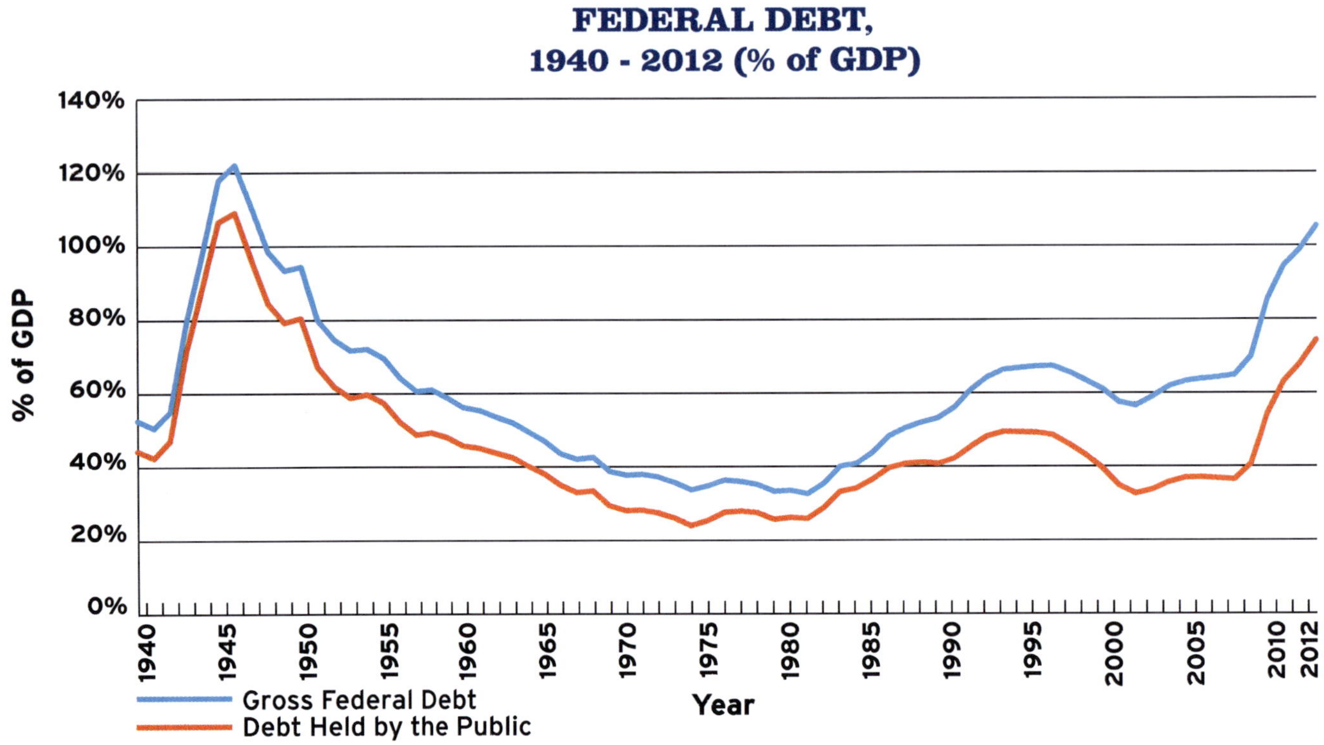

FIGURE 4 SOURCE: Budget of the U.S. Government FY 2013, http://www.gpo.gov/fdsys/pkg/BUDGET-2013-TAB/xls/BUDGET-2013-TAB-7-1.xls.

DEBT IN THE OBAMA ADMINISTRATION

When President Obama was sworn into office on January 20, 2009, the U.S. had a total of $10.6 trillion in debt outstanding, according to the Treasury Department's Bureau of the Public Debt. For the reasons described above, the debt has increased precipitously since then. In fact, as of January 2, 2013, the U.S. government had a total of $11.6 trillion in debt held by the public and $4.86 trillion in intra-governmental holdings, for a total of $16.4 trillion in outstanding debt. This represents a 55 percent increase in gross debt in less than four years.

According to renowned studies by economists Kenneth Rogoff and Carmen Reinhart, a country faces substantial barriers to economic growth when the ratio of sovereign debt to GDP reaches 90 percent. This scholarship has been challenged by some, but it is widely accepted.

From one perspective, then, the U.S. has accrued too much debt. At the end of FY 2011, gross federal debt had reached 98.7 percent of GDP, up from just 69.7 percent at the end of FY 2008. However, some argue that gross debt, which combines debt held by the public and intra-governmental holdings, is not the proper measure to use when calculating the ratio of debt to GDP. Instead, these critics claim that net debt (in other words, only the debt held by the public, and not debt created through intra-governmental transfers) should be used in these calculations. Using this latter method, the debt-to-GDP ratio at the end of FY 2011 was 67.7 percent, well below the cut-off established by Rogoff and Reinhart, and the ratio was expected to rise to no more than 77.1 percent by the end of FY 2017. In these terms, the growth of federal debt appears much less threatening.

The debt has grown so quickly because of large and repeated annual deficits in federal spending. In FY 2009, the fiscal year in which the recent economic crisis was at its worst and in which the federal government spent over $1 trillion in stimulus funding, the deficit was $1.41 trillion, the result of $3.52 trillion in outlays and only $2.11 trillion in receipts. Deficits in FY 2010 and FY 2011 were $1.29 trillion and $1.30 trillion, respectively.

Such large sums are difficult to conceptualize properly. To put the situation in perspective, if the federal government spent its yearly revenues exclusively on debt reduction and ceased all of its operations, it would take three or four years to pay down all the debt. Or, the government could pay down the debt in one blow if it simply took more than $52,000 from every person living in the U.S., including children, the elderly, and the unemployed. If this one-time "debt reduction fee" were levied only on those in the workforce, the cost would be over $106,000 per person.

From another perspective, cutting spending on commonly targeted programs is unlikely to resolve the problem. Deficit hawks often call for cuts to what they describe as unnecessary federal programs like the National Endowment for the Arts. However, the NEA's bill is actually quite small. At today's funding levels, the Endowment could operate for more than 100,000 years before it ran up a bill as large as the current federal debt.

THE BENEFITS OF DEBT

Though current levels of federal spending may seem alarming, with trillion-dollar deficits and rapidly rising gross debt, it is important to remember that federal debt serves a valid purpose in ensuring a functional government. Alexander Hamilton famously recognized this when serving as the first U.S. Secretary of the Treasury. In 1781, when the young country was facing the challenge of repaying debts created during the Revolutionary War, Hamilton wrote, "A national debt, if it is not excessive, will be to us a national blessing." He argued that by incurring and then paying off debts a country could build a reputation as a safe haven for investors. This faith would then allow the government to raise large amounts of money very quickly in times of need, such as wars or economic crises, through the sale of government bonds.

Similarly, some economists today believe that government spending in a time of economic recession is a good thing, even when it leads to significant increases in debt and deficit. Paul Krugman, one of the most adamant proponents of this Keynesian economic doctrine, has argued that the ballooning of government deficit and debt is not yet a reason to worry. By stimulating demand through increased spending, Krugman has argued, the government can stimulate economic growth. This will set the nation back on the path of economic growth, allowing the government to repay the debts it had incurred.

WHAT NOW?

Given today's fiscal circumstances, how should the government deal with its debt and its annual balance of receipts and outlays?

Members of the Republican Party, especially those who have aligned themselves with the "Tea Party," believe that the government should severely curtail its spending. A common cry among these groups is that "the government has a spending problem, not a revenue problem." It is this fiscal ideology that led to sequestration, the deep across-the-board cuts that went into effect on March 1, 2013. These policies are also reflected in the fiscally conservative House budget, which was drafted in large part by Representative Paul Ryan (R-WI), chairman of the House Budget Committee. It is interesting to note that these plans generally call for substantial cuts in spending but do not raise taxes, which would also reduce the federal debt.

On the other hand, many politicians and economists argue that drastic reductions in federal spending would be harmful at this time, when the economy is still recovering. They claim that federal spending is needed to spur the economic growth that will lead the country out of recession. As evidence, they point to European countries, like Greece, that have enacted austerity measures. Although government outlays have decreased sharply in these countries, economic indicators such as unemployment rates show that their economies continue to struggle. According to the opponents of fiscal conservatives, this demonstrates that cuts in federal spending will not solve the problem.

Even once the decision has been made to cut spending or to raise taxes, though, specific choices will remain difficult.

What programs should be cut? Republicans often suggest cuts to Head Start, Medicaid, and other "social safety net" programs; Democrats argue that these cuts would unfairly harm those in most need of assistance. On the other hand, Democrats regularly call for cuts in spending on defense and homeland security; Republicans counter that these cuts would result in a country vulnerable to attacks.

What taxes should be raised? An increase in the corporate tax rate could quickly raise billions, but fiscal conservatives argue that this would hurt American businesses and encourage companies to move their jobs overseas. By restoring the individual income tax to its pre-Bush levels, the government could take a substantial chunk out of its debts, but American families would have thousands less to spend every year as a consequence. Alternatively, the government could also levy a new tax, such as a tax on carbon emissions, or increase taxes that are currently low by global standards, such as the federal gasoline tax. But, this would reduce consumption and restrict some productive activities.

The problem is stark, but the answers are far from clear. This project, the Annual Report of the U.S.A., aims to clarify the issues by providing information on federal revenues and outlays that will help American citizens make informed judgments with respect to the federal budget.

★

AMERICA'S FINANCES: NET INTEREST

by Daniel Backman

Just as most people borrow money from a bank when buying a house or a car, the federal government borrows money to pay for the expenditures that it does not fully fund at the time of purchase. In both cases, while paying the lender back, the borrower (either the home buyer or the government) also pays the lender some percentage of the original loan in interest. This interest compensates the lender for the service of providing cash when needed, and it also remunerates the lender for parting with money that he or she could have invested elsewhere (this is called the opportunity cost). In addition, interest rewards the lender for taking the risk that the borrower may not pay back the loan amount in full.

The U.S. government lends and borrows trillions of dollars every year, and it either pays or collects interest on most of these loans. To borrow money, the Department of the Treasury issues Treasury securities: Treasury bills, Treasury bonds, Treasury notes, and Treasury Inflation-Protected Securities (TIPS). Treasuries, as such securities are often called, represent a loan from the buyer to the U.S. government. The period of time between purchase of a Treasury and repayment, known as the security's maturity, ranges from one month to 30 years.[1]

The U.S. government also receives interest payments on loans and investments it makes. For example, the federal government earned an estimated $1.3 billion in interest on loans made to states to help fund their unemployment benefit programs during FY 2012.[2]

Together, the interest paid on Treasury securities and the returns made on loans and investments comprise the net interest component of the federal budget. For at least 70 years, the government has paid more in interest than it has received.[3]

Treasuries are used to finance both the government's annual budget deficits and the federal debt. Consequently, it is not possible to talk about net interest without talking about the national debt.

NET INTEREST AND THE NATIONAL DEBT: A BRIEF HISTORY

Since its earliest days, the United States has financed its government operations in part by issuing debt. In 1776, the Continental Army funded its fight against the British by borrowing from France and the Netherlands. In 1789, Alexander Hamilton, the first Secretary of the Treasury, wrote that "a national debt, if not excessive, will be to us a national blessing."[4] Indeed, with the singular exception of a few months after January 1835, the United States has owed interest on debt for its entire history as a nation.[5]

Historical records demonstrate the relationship between the national debt and net interest, which is largely made up of the interest paid on that debt. Figure 5 shows both publicly held debt and net interest owed as a percent of GDP.[6]

1 "Federal Debt and Interest Costs," Congressional Budget Office, December 2010: 6.
2 "Analytical Perspectives, Budget of the United States Government, Fiscal Year 2013," Office of Management and Budget, February 13, 2012: Table 32-1.
3 "Fiscal Year 2012 Historical Tables," Office of Management and Budget, 2011.
4 "The 18th Century," Bureau of the Public Debt, http://www.publicdebt.treas.gov/history/1700.htm.
5 "The 19th Century," Bureau of the Public Debt, http://www.publicdebt.treas.gov/history/1800.htm.
6 "Fiscal Year 2012 Historical Tables," Office of Management and Budget, 2011.

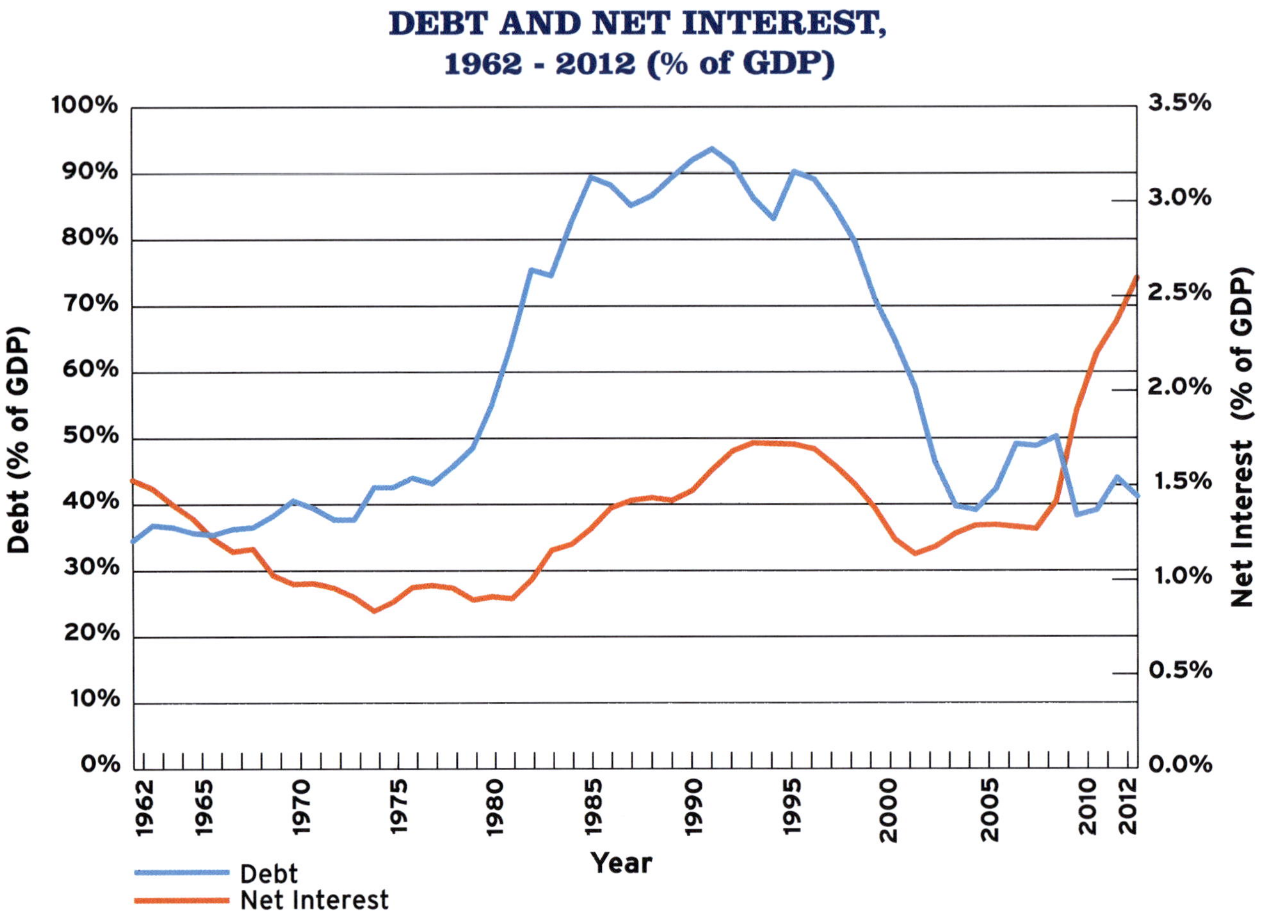

FIGURE 5 SOURCE: Budget of the U.S. Government FY 2013, http://www.gpo.gov/fdsys/pkg/BUDGET-2013-TAB/xls/BUDGET-2013-TAB-3-2.xls and http://www.gpo.gov/fdsys/pkg/BUDGET-2013-TAB/xls/BUDGET-2013-TAB-7-1.xls.

As this graph shows, there is generally a positive relationship between the size of the national debt and the size of net interest payments. Generally, the more the federal government owes, the more interest it must pay to its lenders. Yet, as this figure also makes clear, the relationship fluctuates.

WHAT DETERMINES NET INTEREST: DEBT, RISK, INFLATION, AND THE MARKET FOR TREASURIES

Size of Debt and Associated Default Risk

When the federal government borrows more money, not only does it pay additional interest because it has taken out a bigger loan, it often has to borrow at a higher interest rate. That occurs because, as discussed above, the interest rate rewards lenders both for parting with their money and for risking default (in other words, the chance that the borrower will fail to pay back the loan). A potential lender who sees the government increasing its debt may begin to doubt the government's ability to pay the money back. The government must then offer a higher interest rate to get the lender to make the loan. And while the U.S. government is one of the most reliable borrowers in the world, default risk is always present to some degree.

In fact, default risk plays a role in loans throughout the economy. For example, imagine that a man named Greg wants to buy a car, but, like most people, he doesn't have enough money sitting around to pay for the car in cash. So, he applies for a 5-year, $30,000 loan from the local bank. The bank examines his credit, including his income and how much other debt he has, and grants him a loan at 3.0 percent interest compounded annually.

The next day, after impressing his wife with his new ride, Greg decides to buy her a car as well. He goes back to the local bank and applies for another $30,000 loan. But this time, the bank sees that he already has $30,000 in debt, plus interest, and knows there is a greater risk that he won't be able to pay back two loans than just one. This time, the bank grants him a second loan at 4.0 percent annual interest. The increase in interest rate is meant to account for the added risk.

The below table summarizes this example:

TABLE 1 - SCENARIO: GREG'S CAR LOANS

	Interest Rate	Initial Loan Amount (Principal)	Interest Owed After 1 Year*	Interest Owed After 5 Years
Car #1	3%	$30,000.00	$900.00	$4,778.22
Car #2	4%	$30,000.00	$1,200.00	$6,499.59
Total		**$60,000.00**	**$2,100.00**	**$11,277.81**

As the table demonstrates, although Greg doubled his debt by buying a second car, he more than doubled the amount he owed in interest due to the higher interest rate on the second loan.

Inflation and the Market for Treasury Securities

In addition to the amount of outstanding government debt and the associated default risk, two other factors help determine the net interest owed by the federal government: the supply and demand for Treasury securities, and inflation.

The supply of Treasuries depends on how much money the government needs to borrow. The more money the government needs, the more it is willing to pay in interest to encourage investors to lend.

On the other hand, the demand for Treasuries depends on how many people want to buy U.S. debt and where else they could invest their money. When a lot of people want to buy Treasuries, which are seen as very low-risk investments, the government can offer a lower interest rate to borrow the money it needs. Conversely, if interest rates on other investments are attractively high and those investments are not seen as being too risky, the government must offer even higher interest rates to incentivize lenders to buy its debt instead of putting their money elsewhere.

A fourth factor, inflation, also has an effect on interest rates for Treasuries. Inflation is a measure of how much prices are increasing in an economy. For example, if inflation is 2 percent, prices will be 2 percent higher in a year than they are now; in other words, a dollar today can only buy about 98 cents worth of goods a year from now.[7] Thus, a lender would have to charge 2 percent interest just to have the same purchasing power in a year that he has today.

The other determinants of interest rates, such as opportunity cost and default risk, are generally added on top of the inflation rate. This total rate is called the nominal interest rate. The interest rate minus the rate of inflation is called the real interest rate.

NET INTEREST TODAY AND IN THE NEAR FUTURE

In FY 2012, net interest accounted for approximately $224 billion of federal spending.[8] At about 1.4 percent of GDP, that amount is on the lower side by recent historical standards.[9] That is because, despite the large national debt, interest rates in recent years have been extremely low. As interest rates rise to more typical levels, however, net interest is projected to increase by more than 11.0 percent per year from 2014 to 2022.[10]

PROJECTED NET INTEREST AND PUBLIC DEBT, 2011 - 2022 (% of GDP)

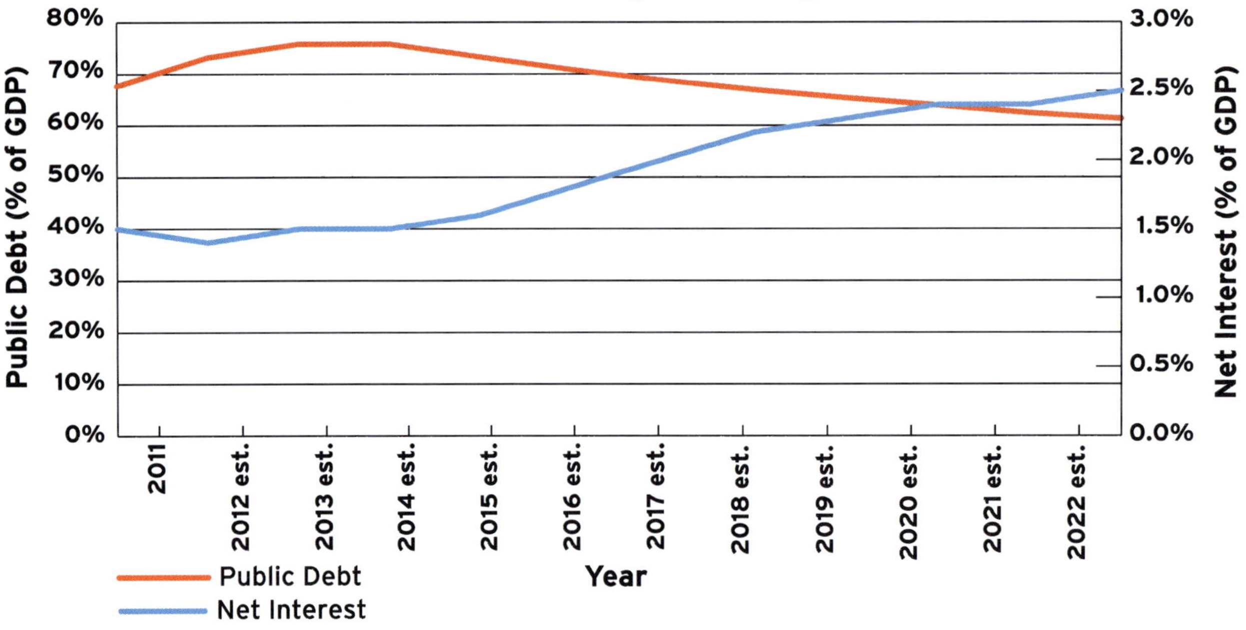

FIGURE 6 SOURCE: Congressional Budget Office, http://www.cbo.gov/sites/default/files/cbofiles/attachments/March2012Baseline.pdf.

Figure 6 illustrates the effect low interest rates have had on net interest.[11] While the debt grew from about 36.0 percent of GDP in 2007 to 73.2 percent of GDP in 2012, net interest as a percentage of GDP actually fell from 1.7 percent to 1.4 percent in that same period. As interest rates rise in the coming years, the national debt is projected to fall from a peak of 75.8 percent of GDP in 2013 to 61.3 percent in 2022 due to budget cuts and a healthier economy. Yet, over that same period, net interest is projected to increase from 1.4 percent of GDP to 2.5 percent.

7 Using the present value formula: 1.00/(1+0.02)^1 = 0.9804.
8 "Analytical Perspectives."
9 "The Budget and Economic Outlook," Congressional Budget Office, February 2012.
10 "The Budget and Economic Outlook," 47.
11 Data from "Historical Tables" (2007-2010) and "Updated Budget Projections: Fiscal Years 2012 to 2022", Congressional Budget Office, March 2012, (2012-2022).

WHY INTEREST RATES ARE SO LOW

Interest rates on Treasury securities today are at historic lows. In 2012, the nominal interest rate on a 3-month Treasury bill was 0.09 percent. Moreover, interest rates throughout the 2000s have been markedly low by historical standards. Figure 7 shows interest rates on 3-month T-bills from January 1934 to December 2012.[12]

INTEREST RATE ON A 3-MONTH TREASURY BILL, 1934 - 2012

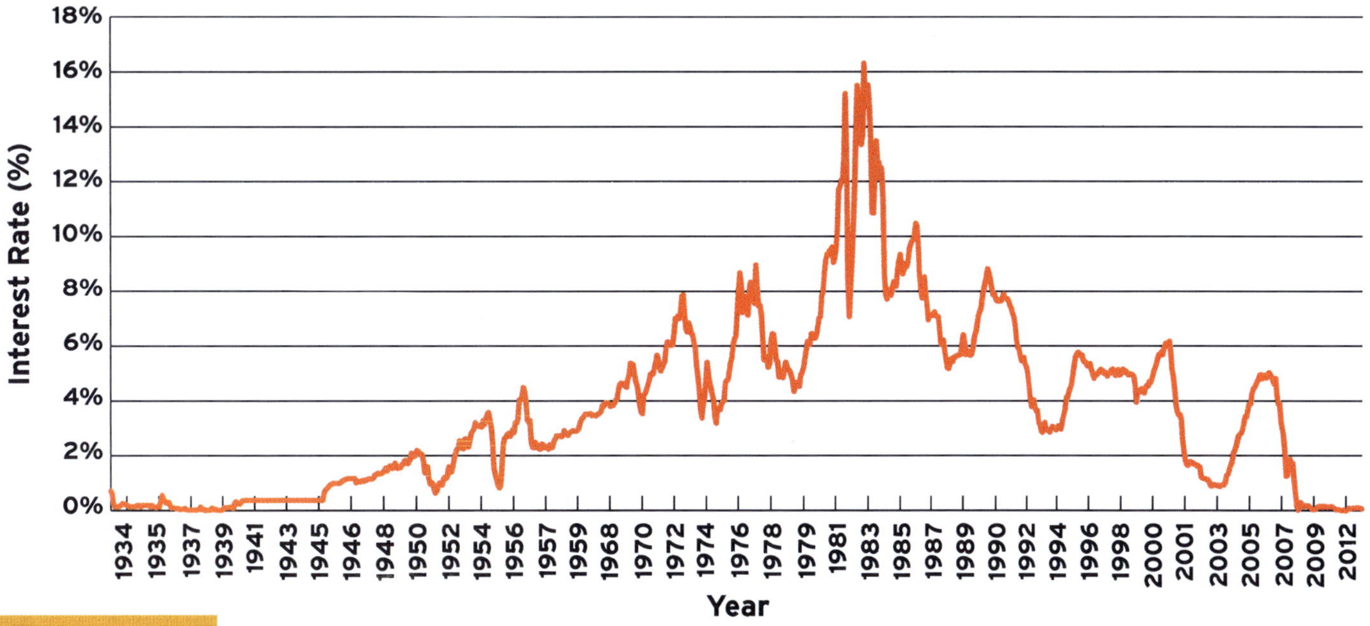

FIGURE 7 SOURCE: Federal Reserve Economic Data, http://research.stlouisfed.org/fred2/series/TB3MS.

As the graph indicates, and as is the case with other maturities as well as many bonds throughout the economy, interest rates on 3-month T-bills are at levels not seen since the Great Depression. Several explanations for these low rates relate to the economic conditions of a severe, protracted recession.

For one, the Federal Reserve will often act to lower market interest rates when the economy is contracting. The Fed's expansionary monetary policy involves, among other actions, buying short-term Treasury bills. With fewer bills remaining on the market, demand increases and the interest rate decreases as a result. The most recent recession saw enormous expansionary efforts by the Fed.[13]

In addition, recessions often come with periods of low inflation, known as disinflation. When consumers want to buy fewer goods than usual, the price of these goods does not increase as quickly. Inflation rates in the 2007-2009 recession were low and, at times, negative (called "deflation").[14] The last major period of disinflation and deflation was, as one might guess, the Great Depression. As discussed above, lower inflation is associated with lower nominal interest rates.

12 Data from the "Federal Reserve Economic Data," Federal Reserve Bank of St. Louis, http://research.stlouisfed.org/fred2/.
13 To learn more about the Federal Reserve's monetary policy tools, see http://www.frbsf.org/publications/federalreserve/fedinbrief/guides.html.
14 "Consumer Price Index," Bureau of Labor Statistics, 2012, ftp://ftp.bls.gov/pub/special.requests/cpi/cpiai.txt.

Finally, since U.S. Treasuries are perceived as a virtually risk-free asset, investors often rush to buy Treasuries when investing elsewhere seems too risky. Times of high risk, including recessions, tend to increase the demand for Treasuries and further lower the interest rate. In the 2008 global financial crisis, not only Americans but also investors worldwide flocked to U.S. Treasuries to keep their money safe from rampant risk across the globe. Europe's subsequent sovereign debt crisis only exacerbated this trend.

WHEN INTEREST RATES REMAIN LOW

What has generated greater debate, however, is the extended period of low interest rates in the early 2000s. After the recession of 2001-2002, the economy began growing again, but interest rates, which traditionally follow growth, remained low. Two competing theories seek to explain this phenomenon.

One, put forth by Stanford economist John Taylor, claims that the Federal Reserve intentionally kept interest rates abnormally low in order to feed economic growth. According to Taylor, given the levels of unemployment and inflation, the Fed should have targeted higher interest rates during much of this period.[15]

> **"The unusually low interest rate decisions were, of course, made with careful consideration by monetary policy makers. One can interpret them as purposeful deviations from the 'regular' interest rate settings based on the usual macroeconomic variables." –John Taylor**

Alternatively, the current chairman of the Federal Reserve, Ben Bernanke, attributed lower interest rates on many global assets, including U.S. Treasury securities, to excessive global saving that increased the supply of loanable funds and lowered interest rates on these assets. In 2005, Bernanke postulated the existence of a "global saving glut" that led to high savers in developing countries purchasing assets in industrialized nations like the United States, thereby dampening interest rates.[16]

> **"[O]ver the past decade a combination of diverse forces has created a significant increase in the global supply of saving—a global saving glut—which helps to explain...the relatively low level of long-term real interest rates in the world today." –Ben Bernanke**

NET INTEREST AND THE SPECTER OF DEFAULT

Still, economists and policymakers generally agree that recent low interest rates should not be taken as a sign that the national debt can continue to grow indefinitely. As previously noted, the CBO expects interest rates to increase as the economy recovers. Further, depending on the policy choices Congress and the President make, investors may begin to perceive increased default risk on Treasuries and demand higher rates.

To gain a better understanding of default risk, recall the above story about Greg and the car loans. The interest Greg owed more than doubled when he doubled the amount he borrowed. As shown in Table 1, Greg's total indebtedness after five years also more than doubled with the purchase of an second car, from $34,800 to $71,300.

15 John B. Taylor, "The Financial Crisis and the Policy Responses: An Empirical Analysis of What Went Wrong," A Festschrift in Honor of David Dodge, Bank of Canada, November 2008.
16 Ben S. Bernanke, "The Global Saving Glut and the U.S. Current Account Deficit," Virginia Association of Economists, Richmond, VA, April 14, 2005.

If Greg tried to get a third loan, banks would respond to his additional debt load by charging an even higher interest rate. This cycle of increased debt leading to increased interest rates and increased debts through interest payments would make the likelihood of Greg defaulting ever greater.

Some economists and policymakers fear a similarly inexorable fate for the U.S. federal government. This has already happened to some extent in Europe. Large debt buildups in Greece and other countries on the Euro common currency have led to increased borrowing costs. These costs have in turn raised the specter of default and further fueled the rise in interest rates.

As macroeconomist and Harvard Kennedy School professor Jeffrey Frankel said, "The arithmetic of the interest payments can turn an apparently sustainable fiscal situation into an explosive path very quickly. This is extremely hard to reverse once it happens." Frankel argued that the best way for governments to avoid this fate is to cut deficits in years of healthy economic growth to compensate for deficits amassed in recessionary years.

"The only solution is to take the opportunity of the upswing of the business cycle to run strong budgets, preferably surpluses. This is what the U.S. did in the late 1990s," explained Frankel. "But the U.S., along with the U.K. and [the Euro zone] forgot this basic principle during the years 2003 to 2007. Now we are all beginning to pay the price."[17]

Two other economists, Carmen Reinhart of the University of Maryland and Kenneth Rogoff of Harvard University, studied eight centuries of sovereign debt and financial crises to further inform the debate. "Those who would point to low servicing costs should remember that market interest rates can change like the weather," they concluded. "Debt levels, by contrast, can't be brought down quickly. Even though politicians everywhere like to argue that their country will expand its way out of debt, our historical research suggests that growth alone is rarely enough to achieve that with the debt levels we are experiencing today."[18]

Still, Princeton economist Paul Krugman has maintained that U.S. politicians should presently focus on growing the economy rather than shrinking the deficit. In reference to the Euro crisis, he wrote that "what Greek experience actually shows is that while running deficits in good times can get you in trouble... Trying to eliminate deficits once you're already in trouble is a recipe for depression."[19]

Further, Krugman has argued that the cycle described above, in which rising debt leads to a higher perceived risk of default and, consequently, even higher interest costs, is not inevitable. To support this claim, Krugman noted that Britain and the U.S. pay lenders at an interest rate of 2 percent, while Japan, which is even more indebted than Greece, pays only 1 percent interest.[20]

★

17 Jeffrey Frankel, e-mail message to author, June 11, 2012.
18 Carmen Reinhart and Kenneth Rogoff, "Too Much Debt Means the Economy Can't Grow: Reinhart and Rogoff," Bloomberg, July 13, 2011, http://www.bloomberg.com/news/2011-07-14/too-much-debt-means-economy-can-t-grow-commentary-by-reinhart-and-rogoff.html.
19 Paul Krugman, "What Greece Means," *The New York Times*, March 11, 2011, http://www.nytimes.com/2012/03/12/opinion/krugman-what-greece-means.html.
20 Paul Krugman, "What Ails Europe?" *The New York Times*, February 26, 2012, http://www.nytimes.com/2012/02/27/opinion/krugman-what-ails-europe.html.

by Matt Shuham

HOW DOES THE GOVERNMENT EARN MONEY?

There are two types of federal revenue: tax revenue and non-tax revenue. While non-tax revenue, including government activity such as investments in private corporations or sales of government property, contributes to some of the government's annual "income," the overwhelming majority of federal revenue comes from taxes.

There are many different types of taxes levied by the U.S. federal government, and trying to explain them all would fill thousands of books. (Indeed, it already has. Just check your local library's section on "tax law.") So, instead of going into every minute detail of the government's tax revenue, this article covers the most important parts of the tax code, including the effects of the recession.

BREAKING DOWN THE TAX SYSTEM: THE BASICS

The President's budget proposal for FY 2013 included $2.9 trillion in revenue.[21] That money comes from a few major sources, listed in the pie graph below:

SOURCES OF FEDERAL REVENUE, FY 2013 (proposed)

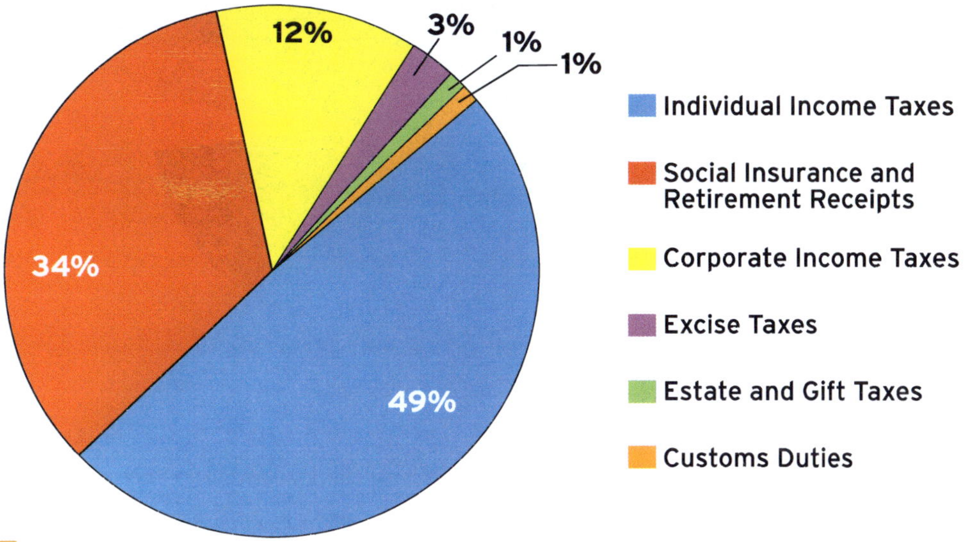

FIGURE 8 SOURCE: Budget of the U.S. Government FY 2013. http://www.whitehouse.gov/sites/default/files/omb/budget/fy2013/assets/budget.pdf.

As is clear from the graph, most federal revenue comes from three sources: individual income taxes, payroll taxes, and corporate income taxes.

THE "BIG THREE"

The "Big Three" accounted for more than 90 percent of revenue in the FY 2013 budget, projected to raise $2.67 trillion, a very large number despite the trials of a half-decade recession, a warren of tax loopholes, and ever-shifting patterns of employment. Upon examination, these three taxes reveal a great deal about the broader economic and political state of America today.

21 "Budget of the U.S. Government," Office of Management and Budget, February 13, 2012, http://www.gpo.gov/fdsys/pkg/BUDGET-2013-BUD/pdf/BUDGET-2013-BUD.pdf.

Individual Income Tax: $1.359 Trillion (49 Percent)

The income tax is the largest single source of federal revenue. It was first enacted in 1861 as a way to pay for the Civil War. At that time, it was a 3 percent tax on all incomes over $800. Later, the income tax was made constitutional through the Sixteenth Amendment, which was passed by Congress in 1909 and ratified in 1913. Now, both incomes and taxes are quite a bit higher, and the income tax code itself is much more complex.

The U.S. has a progressive income tax system, meaning that people with large incomes pay a higher percentage of their income in taxes than people with low incomes, who may in fact pay no taxes or receive payment from the government as a result of filing their tax returns.

Following the American Taxpayer Relief Act of 2012 (ATRA), which was passed by Congress in early January 2013, there are seven different tax brackets based on income:

TABLE 2 - TAX BRACKETS AFTER ATRA

Marginal Tax Rate	Single	Married, Filing Jointly	Head of Household
10%	$0 to $8,925	$0 to $17,850	$0 to $12,750
15%	$8,925 to $36,250	$17,850 to $72,500	$12,750 to $48,600
25%	$36,250 to $87,850	$72,500 to $146,400	$48,600 to $125,450
28%	$87,850 to $183,250	$146,400 to $223,050	$125,450 to $203,150
33%	$183,250 to $398,350	$223,050 to $398,350	$203,150 to $398,350
35%	$398,350 to $400,000	$398,350 to $450,000	$398,350 to $425,000
39.6%	Over $400,000	Over $450,000	Over $425,000

These tax rates are marginal, meaning that they apply only to the portion of the person's income that falls in the bracket. For example, a single person who makes $75,000 in a year will pay $14,678.75 in federal taxes—10 percent on income between $0 and $8,925 ($892.50), 15 percent on income between $8,925 and $36,250 ($4,098.75), and 25 percent on income between $36,250 and $75,000 ($9,687.50).

To give another example, a married person who files jointly with a spouse and has an income of $50,000 will pay $6,607.50 in federal taxes—10 percent on income up to $17,850 ($1,785.00) and 15 percent on income between $17,850 and $50,000 ($4,822.50).

As with many other sources of revenue, income tax revenue was significantly affected by the recession, primarily because there were fewer people paying taxes. In addition, with more people working part-time jobs or for lower wages, more people began to qualify for the Earned Income Tax Credit (EITC), a fully refundable tax credit that drastically reduces or even eliminates individual tax liability.[22]

This is the reason that arguments over the national debt inevitably touch on employment: more employment means more tax revenue. Similarly, the arguments over employment often find their way back to tax policy, precisely because there are many different views on which tax structures facilitate healthy, growing economies.

22 Chuck Marr and Chye-Ching Huang, "Misconceptions and Realities about Who Pays Taxes," Center on Budget and Policy Priorities, April 11,2012, http://www.cbpp.org/cms/index.cfm?fa=view&id=3505.

Great Debate: Paying a Fair Share

The most modern rendition of the debate on income tax fairness came with President Obama's inauguration. Almost immediately, he was faced with the decision of whether or not to extend the tax cuts signed into law by the George W. Bush administration. President Obama ultimately did sign these cuts into law, but only unwillingly, and after a drawn-out political battle and aggressive rhetoric from conservative legislators.

The main point of contention was over the "top marginal tax rate," which in Table 2 is the lowest row—now 39.6 percent due to the American Taxpayer Relief Act of 2012, though just 35 percent under the Bush tax cut system. Conservatives argue that lower tax rates, especially on wealthier individuals, should encourage job growth and economic expansion. According to them, the knowledge that government will ultimately take less of a citizen's money in taxes is an incentive for that citizen to work harder and hire more employees. On its face, this makes perfect sense. But during the Bush presidency, these supposed outcomes could hardly be seen. In fact, it seemed that these tax cuts did little more than enlarge the national debt.

There's another side of the coin, though. In 2011, President Obama announced his new "Buffet Act." The proposal took its name from billionaire investor Warren Buffet, who has observed that he pays taxes at a lower rate than his secretary and has advocated higher taxes for the wealthy. Accordingly, the proposal put forth the economic ideology that America's wealthiest should, for reasons of fairness and revenue generation, pay taxes at a higher rate than they currently do. It would ensure that people earning more than a million dollars annually are required to pay a minimum 30 percent effective tax rate. Again, the word "effective" is key. As with corporations, wealthy individuals often take advantage of tax credits, offshore accounts, and other loopholes that make their taxable income much lower, resulting in a low effective tax rate even thought their statutory tax rate may be 39.6 percent. This is how Buffet's secretary ended up paying taxes at a higher rate than her boss.

Millionaires are not common, and the Buffet Rule would only affect approximately 0.3 percent of taxpayers in the U.S. Since so few would be affected by it, it would only account for a small percentage of total revenue. Estimates for how much the Buffet Rule would raise range from as much as $50 billion a year, according to Citizens for Tax Justice, to as little as $46.7 billion over the next decade, according to the Joint Committee on Taxation. Overall, the potential increase in revenue is small compared to the amount of attention that Congress and commentators alike are giving it.

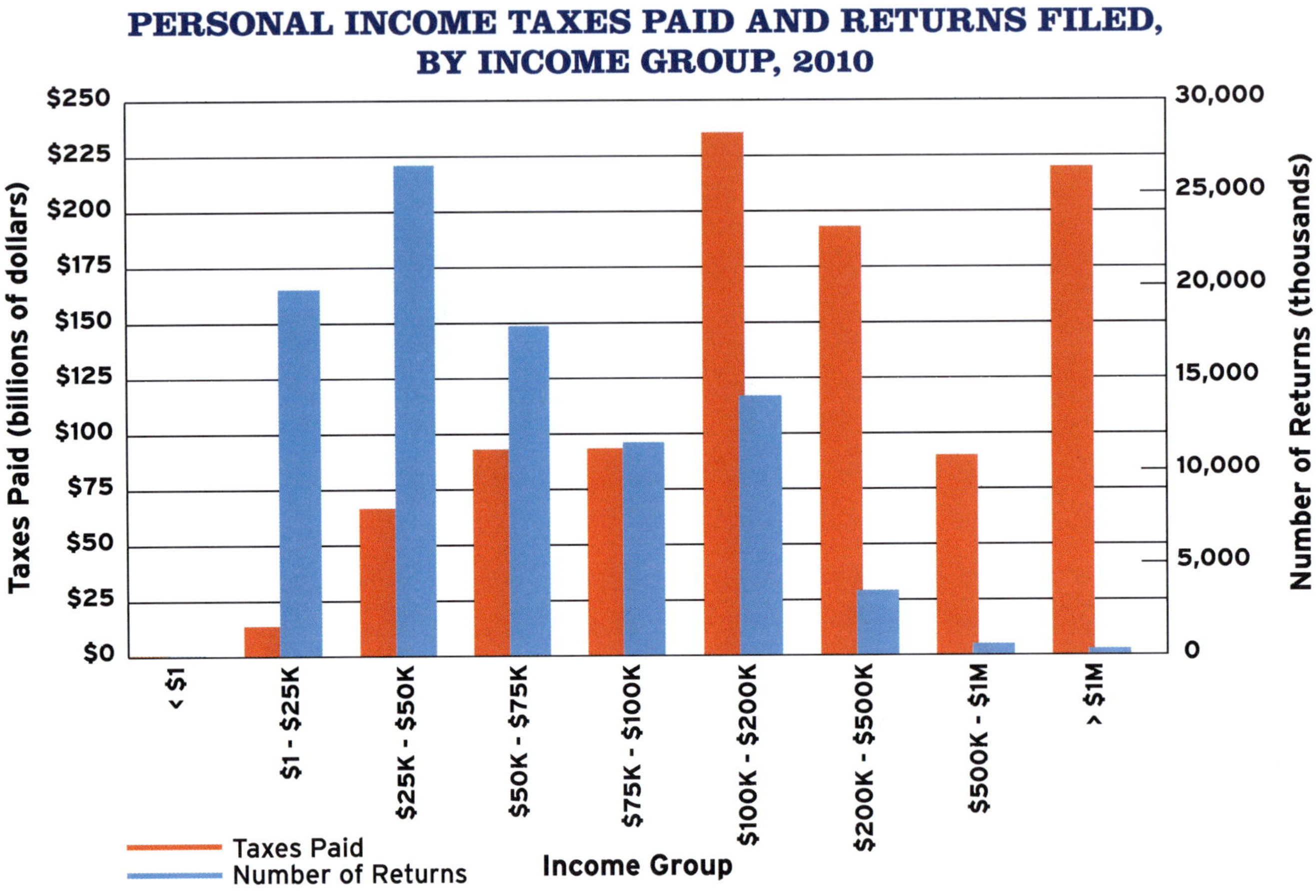

FIGURE 9 SOURCE: Internal Revenue Service, http://www.irs.gov/file_source/pub/irs-soi/10in53us.xls.

Payroll Taxes: $959 Billion (34 Percent)

The term "payroll taxes" denotes two types of taxes. First, employers withhold a certain amount of an employee's paycheck automatically in order to pay for Medicare and Social Security. Second, employers must also pay federal taxes for each of their employees, beyond the gross salaries paid to workers. Currently, 6.2 percent of employee wages are withheld for a Social Security tax, and 1.45 percent of wages are withheld for a Medicare tax. (Until ATRA, employees paid only 4.2 percent of wages for the Social Security tax.) Employers must pay 6.2 percent of employee gross income for the Social Security tax and 1.45 percent for the Medicare tax.

Great Debate: Payroll Taxes and the Solvency of our Entitlement Programs

The relationship between payroll taxes and the very programs that they fund, Medicare and Social Security, has been a prominent political issue over the past year. To understand the debate, it's crucial to understand the history of these entitlement programs.

The Social Security program began in 1935 as a part of President Franklin D. Roosevelt's New Deal program. Then, as now, Social Security acted to combat poverty among the elderly. Medicare was added to Social Security in 1965 as a way to assist with health care payments, one of the biggest expenses Americans face in old age. Social

Security is funded through FICA, the Federal Insurance Contributions Act, which was written into the IRS tax code in 1939.

Herein lies some of the problem: FICA collects taxes from current workers, but Social Security is a program meant for retirees. Thus, workers pay now for the benefits that they'll receive later. This becomes a problem if, for example, there are many more retirees than there are workers paying the FICA tax. The tax revenue collected from the smaller number of workers wouldn't satisfy the total Social Security burden that the government has for the large number of retirees. In fact, this is exactly what's happening now, as the "Baby Boomer" generation reaches retirement.

In 2010, for the first time, the U.S. government paid out more money to Social Security recipients than it took in.[23]

There are a few options that would, at the very least, lessen the problem.

First, through privatization, current seniors would be given money to invest privately. Meanwhile, the federal government would be left to make tough choices about how to pay for the large debts that Social Security has already racked up and about how to pay for future generations. Liberals tend to oppose the idea because it would leave large numbers of seniors vulnerable not only to the unpredictable activity of stock markets but also to potential exploitation in the private market by predatory lenders and investors. Furthermore, current and future generations would ultimately have to foot the bill.

Second, the government could implement massive reform. "Fixing" the way Americans pay, collect, and distribute payroll taxes is a daunting proposition. The sheer complexity of the task often encourages legislators to ignore the problem and leave it for future generations to confront. Still, common sense says that money cannot be created or destroyed without effects: entitlement programs must either collect more, give out less, or carry out a combination of the two. Suggestions for massive reform fall along these lines: raise the taxes on current workers, raise the retirement age from the current threshold (from 65 to 67 years of age, depending on year of birth), or lower benefits for wealthy retirees. But because the elderly are such a large and reliable voting bloc, politicians are hesitant to take on the issue with full force.

Great Debate: The Difference 2 Percent Makes, or, the Story Behind the "Payroll Tax Cut"

In 2011, the Social Security tax for employees was 4.2 percent, 2 percentage points lower than it was the year before. That was because President Obama signed the Tax Hike Prevention Act of 2010 in December 2010. Among a whole slew of tax cuts and write-offs, the law cut the employee OASDI ("Old-Age, Survivors, and Disability Insurance," more commonly known as Social Security) tax by two percentage points. Two percentage points might not seem like much, but it made a large difference.

In 2012, Democrats fought hard to have the payroll tax cut extended. They argued that during a recession giving extra tax benefits to consumers would boost spending. Republicans briefly argued that keeping the tax cut wasn't a wise move long term (these two are ironic flip-flops from standard partisan tax policies, incidentally). In the

23 Mary Williams Walsh, "Social Security to See Payout Exceed Pay-In This Year," *The New York Times*, March 24, 2010, http://www.nytimes.com/2010/03/25/business/economy/25social.html.

end, both were somewhat right: consumer spending probably went up more than it would have without the 2 percentage point tax cut, but Social Security wasn't any better off in the long run thanks to losing billions of dollars in potential revenue.

Ultimately, in ATRA, the payroll tax cut was not extended and the Social Security tax on employees was restored to its previous rate of 6.2 percent.

COMPOSITION OF FEDERAL TAXES, 1934 - 2012

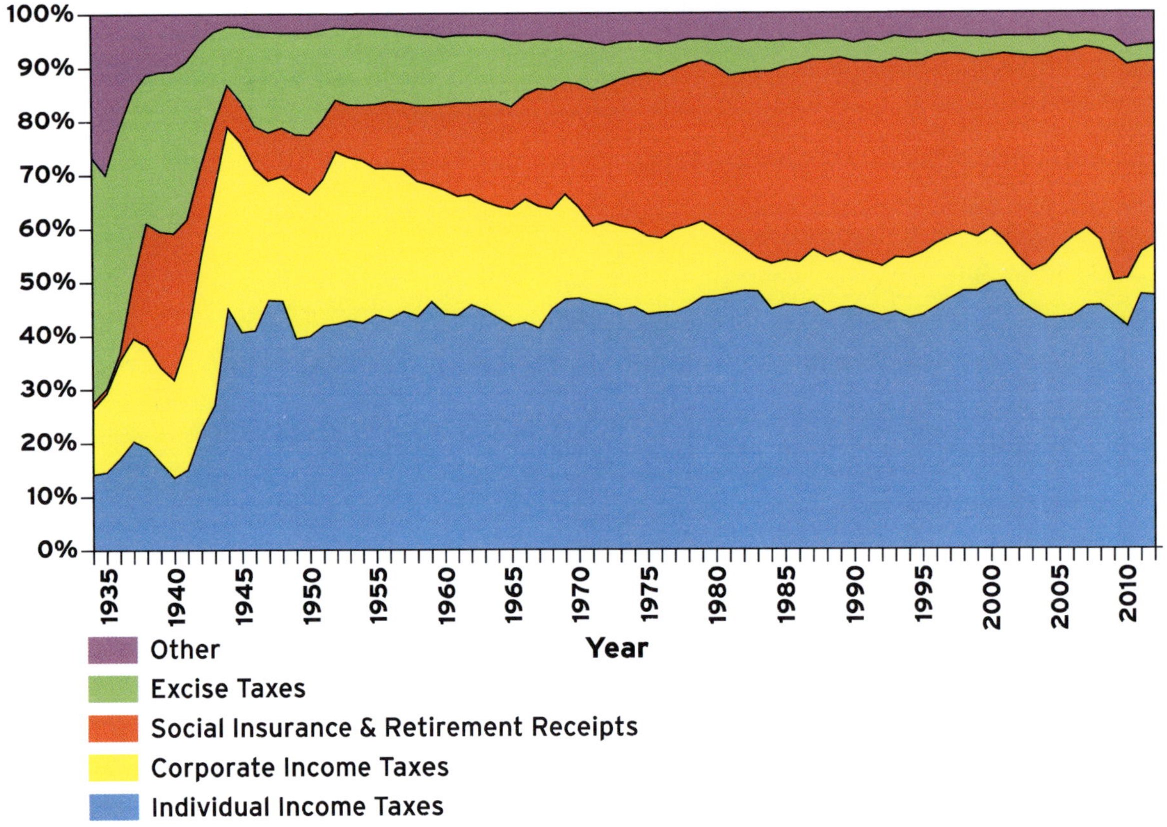

FIGURE 10 SOURCE: Budget of the U.S. Government FY 2013, http://www.gpo.gov/fdsys/pkg/BUDGET-2013-TAB/xls/BUDGET-2013-TAB-2-1.xls.

Corporate Income Tax: $348 Billion (12 Percent)

The corporate tax is paid by businesses on certain types of revenue. The entire code of what revenue is and is not taxed is fairly complex, but it basically breaks down to this: standard profit from selling goods or services ("net revenue") is taxed. From this, businesses can subtract a number of tax deductions, or activities that produce revenue yet are exempt from taxes. Examples include hiring extra workers, creating manufacturing plants in the U.S., and using environmentally friendly technology. In fact, there are so many available tax deductions available in the corporate tax code that some businesses pay close to nothing in corporate taxes.[24]

24 Felix Salmon, "Charts of the day, corporate income-tax edition," Reuters, November 17, 2011, http://blogs.reuters.com/felix-salmon/2011/11/17/charts-of-the-day-corporate-income-tax-edition/.

It is worth noting that corporate tax revenue reveals a great deal about the state of the American economy. Businesses that are doing poorly, especially those with net losses rather than net gains over the course of a fiscal year, often do not pay any corporate tax at all. This is because the corporate tax is somewhat progressive, meaning that companies earning less have to pay a smaller percentage of their income in taxes. For example, a company in 2011 with less than $50,000 in taxable income only had to pay a 15 percent top marginal tax rate on its income. Meanwhile, a company making more than $18.3 million had to pay taxes at a 35 percent top marginal rate.

It's important to note that "taxable income" is by no means the same thing as "income." As was mentioned in the beginning of this section, companies can get tax breaks for many or most their business expenses. As a result, even though the lowest corporate tax rate is nominally 15 percent and not 0 percent, many companies end up paying no corporate income taxes. In fact, from 1998 to 2005, 55 percent of large corporations paid no income tax.

Great Debate: The Loophole Game

These deductions and credits, called "tax breaks" or "loopholes" by critics, result in a discrepancy between nominal and effective tax rates. Along these lines, there seems to be an ongoing argument between Democrats and Republicans in the federal government as to what should and should not be considered taxable income.

As part of their daily operations, corporations across America make investments in certain things—such as labor, equipment, and research and development—that they do not think should be subject to taxation. They also perform certain functions in society—such as working with charitable organizations and performing *pro bono* work—that they feel should entitle them to a lower tax rate. Most people agree, therefore, that certain actions, investments, and earnings should be tax exempt, if only as an incentive to promote the public good.

The status of some activities, however, is not so clear. In 2010, Whirlpool paid no taxes, mostly because of so-called "green credits," or tax incentives for creating energy-efficient consumer appliances. According to a *Wall Street Journal* report, "Whirlpool has stockpiled more than $500 million in tax credits for making energy-saving 'Energy Star' appliances—washers, dryers, refrigerators and so on. The firm gets a production tax credit of up to $200 per refrigerator, $75 per dishwasher, and $225 per washer and dryer."[25] Though energy-efficient appliances have some social benefits, whether or not their producers should be completely exempt from taxation is debatable.

The loopholes extend far beyond fairly innocent examples of incentivizing environmental friendliness. Oftentimes, large corporations take advantage of the complexity of global markets by reporting to the IRS that they already pay taxes abroad. (The U.S. tax system does not include corporate revenue that has already been taxed by an overseas government, thus avoiding "double taxation.") At the same time, these corporations tell foreign governments that they are paying taxes elsewhere. Thus, billions go untaxed.[26] Worse still, large corporations are able to pay millions of dollars for legal and lobbying assistance in order to affect legislation so that the tax code continues to allow for such deductions and credits.

25 "Tax Reform Exhibit A: How Whirlpool parlays green credits into zero tax liability," *Wall Street Journal*, March 3, 2011, http://online.wsj.com/article/SB10001424052748704506004576174321393436988.html.

26 Ann McFeatters, "Tax loopholes leak billions in revenue," *Daily Republic*, January 18, 2012, http://www.dailyrepublic.com/opinion/statenationalcolumnists/tax-loopholes-leak-billions-in-revenue/.

Possible solutions to the loophole problem—and, by extension, possible sources of billions of dollars in government revenue—are varied and numerous. Some reformers argue for radically changing the tax code, ridding it of all but the most essential tax exemptions, such as those for religious institutions and charitable giving. This is easier said than done.

OTHER MAJOR TAXES

In addition to the Big Three taxes, there are three other federal taxes of note: excise taxes, customs duties, and estate and gift taxes.

Excise Taxes and Customs Duties: $88 Billion and $33 Billion

Excise taxes and customs duties are both taxes on products. The difference between the two is that excise taxes are "inland" taxes, meaning they are levied on products bought within the U.S., while customs duties are "border" taxes, meaning they are levied on products imported into the U.S. Examples of excise taxes include cigarette taxes and fuel taxes. An example of a customs duty is the duty placed on t-shirts imported from China.

While excise taxes and customs duties are often seen as purely a source of government revenue, the federal government also uses them as tools for social and economic change. For example, excise taxes on cigarettes, gasoline, and alcohol also serve to discourage the use of these products. In the same vein, customs duties are often levied to encourage Americans to buy domestically manufactured products, because these duties are ultimately transferred to the consumer in the form of higher prices for foreign goods. These two revenue sources accounted for $121 billion of the President's FY 2013 budget proposal.

Estate and Gift Taxes: $13 Billion

Estate and gift taxes are both taxes on the transfer of property. An estate tax applies to inheritances passed down by a deceased person to his inheritors, and a gift tax applies to gifts given while both the giver and receiver are living. In other words, the difference between the estate and gift tax is, to put it gently, the vitality of the parties involved.

The estate tax is one of the most contentious taxes in American politics today. Liberals often view the estate tax as an important tool in guarding against so-called "American Dynasties" such as those common in the Gilded Age. Far-left Democrats would describe lavish wills as inherently unfair because they give an automatic leg-up to those born into wealth. Opposite that, Conservatives often derogatively refer to the estate tax as the "death tax" and consider it a punishment for being successful in life. Like many other taxes, the Right considers the estate tax a disincentive to economic success. In 2010, as a result of congressional action under George W. Bush's leadership, the estate tax disappeared entirely, though it was re-instated the following year.

THE EFFECTS OF A RECESSION: AN ECONOMIST ROUNDTABLE

Recessions are especially damaging with respect to tax revenue. Businesses are less certain about their economic futures, so they are more reserved in their hiring and investments. Employees regularly see wage cuts from flailing employers, resulting in less payroll and income tax revenue. There are also some outcomes that are more difficult to estimate: How many new businesses would have started if the recession hadn't made the economy so unstable? How many more workers would have been hired if employers weren't concerned about conditions worsening?

To get a clearer view of the recession's impact on tax revenue, ARUSA sought perspectives from three experts: Donald Marron, Director of the Urban-Brookings Tax Policy Center; Benjamin Friedman, William Joseph Maier Professor of Political Economy at Harvard University; and Chad Stone, Chief Economist at the Center on Budget and Policy Priorities.

How do large economic events like the burst of the housing bubble and subsequent recession affect government tax revenues?

Benjamin Friedman: "Most of the federal government's taxes are based on incomes, payrolls or profits. When a speculative bubble ends and asset prices go down, firms make less profit (some go out of business), they employ fewer workers, and those with jobs earn less."

Donald Marron: "All of those have a direct effect on tax revenues, one that is magnified by the progressive structure of income tax rates (i.e., when times are good, more income tends to fall in higher tax brackets)."

Chad Stone: "In fact, changes in revenue tend to be larger than changes in income, so the loss of revenue in a deep and protracted recession can add substantially to the budget deficit and debt even if there have been no changes in tax rates or tax laws. Similarly, in an expansion, revenues grow more quickly than income and the budget deficit declines even without any change in tax rates or tax laws."

How are different revenue sources affected? What are the different effects on income tax, payroll tax, and corporate tax revenue streams, respectively?

Chad Stone: "Corporate profits tend to be a more volatile component of income than wages, falling sharply in economic downturns and rising quickly in economic expansions. So corporate income tax revenues tend to have fairly wide swings over the business cycle compared with individual income tax revenues. Some of the volatility in the individual income tax comes from the progressive rate structure. Not only does taxable income fall in a recession, but less of total taxable income is in the higher tax brackets. Payroll taxes show the least variability because they tend to have flat or regressive rates."

Donald Marron: "Income taxes tend to be particularly volatile for several reasons. First, as noted above, the federal rate structure is progressive. When incomes weaken, income tax revenues thus decline because incomes fall (relative to what they would have been) and a smaller fraction falls in higher tax brackets. In addition, income taxes on investment returns, particularly capital gains, can be especially volatile—capital gains can dry up quickly in an economic downturn."

How soon can we expect tax revenues to return to pre-recession numbers?

Chad Stone: "It depends on the policies we follow over the next several years. In fiscal year 2007 [before the recession], federal receipts were equal to 18.5 percent of gross domestic product (GDP). Policymakers are unlikely to let all the Bush-era tax cuts expire immediately, especially those for middle-class taxpayers.

[However,] the CBO estimates that if the policies recommended in President Obama's 2013 budget were implemented, with the middle-class tax cuts extended but not the upper income tax cuts as well as some other changes, revenues would be 18.7 percent of GDP in 2014."

Can you clarify the differences between tax rates and tax revenue? Why would we want a "revenue neutral" tax increase or decrease? In your opinion, do politics get in the way of effective tax policy? How so?

Donald Marron: "There are three basic concepts here: revenues, marginal tax rates, and average tax rates.

"To take a simple example, imagine a tax system in which people pay no tax on their first $10,000 of income and 20 percent tax on everything above that.

"Now consider a person who earns $20,000. She would face a marginal tax rate of 20 percent (i.e., she would owe 20 cents for each incremental dollar she earns). She would pay $2,000 in taxes—the tax revenue to the government. And her average (sometimes called effective) tax rate would be 10 percent = $2,000 / $20,000.

"Analysts often focus on marginal tax rates because they are the ones that are most likely to influence behavior—e.g., by discouraging work or encouraging people to take advantage of tax shelters or even to evade taxes. Those effects aren't that big at the 20 percent rate I chose as an example here. But imagine if the rate were 80 percent. That would create a huge incentive for weird behavior.

"So consider a second tax system, in which the first $17,500 of income is exempt from tax, and the remainder is taxed at 80 percent. Our hypothetical person earning $20,000 would face the same tax bill as above: $2,000 = 80 percent x ($20,000 - $17,500). But that 80 percent marginal tax rate would give her a big incentive to lie on her taxes, to work less, etc.

"The rationale for revenue neutral tax reform is that a tax system like the first one is better than the second one because it has lower marginal rates. In order to afford those lower rates, though, the tax base—i.e., the income that gets taxed—has to be larger. In this simple example, that happens with a smaller exception. In the real world, it would happen by rolling back tax expenditures."

★

by Daniel Backman

THE AMERICAN RECOVERY AND REINVESTMENT ACT OF 2009

Late 2008 saw the worst U.S. financial crisis since 1929. In September 2008, after major investment firm Lehman Brothers filed for bankruptcy, the mortgage market unraveled, soon followed by the rest of the financial system. As stocks tumbled, businesses lost confidence, laid off their workers, and started saving their money in preparation for the worst. Banks, suffering huge losses, stopped lending. Gross domestic product, a measure of the economy's output, declined precipitously; unemployment levels rose. The Great Recession had hit.[27]

The Federal government responded with unprecedented measures to mitigate the effects of the financial crisis on the broader economy. Chief among them was the American Recovery and Reinvestment Act of 2009, a $787 billion fiscal stimulus package signed by President Obama on February 17, 2009. The Recovery Act had two main goals: to create and save jobs, and to spur economic growth in both the short- and long-term.[28] To accomplish these goals, the Act provided for direct government spending, tax cuts, grants and loans to states, and transfers to unemployed and struggling individuals.

While the Recovery Act was arguably the largest economic recovery package in U.S. history, it was not the first. Indeed, the concept of the government spending money and cutting taxes to aid a struggling economy goes back to the work of economist John Maynard Keynes in the 1930s. Keynes, writing in the midst of an even worse economic crisis, posited that the government should increase spending during times of below-potential output. By Keynes's theory, the government could make up for declines in investment and consumption by increasing its own spending—or cutting taxes to boost consumption. This theory formed the foundation of the influential Keynesian school of economics.[29]

Keynesian economic ideas have played a major role in policymaking since that time. In fact, 90 percent of economists today agree that fiscal policy (i.e., taxes and/or government spending) "has a significant stimulative impact on a less than fully employed economy."[30] Yet economists, policymakers, and the American public find less agreement about the efficacy of the Recovery Act in particular.

THE RECOVERY ACT BY THE NUMBERS

Initial estimates from the time of the Recovery Act's signing put the total cost at about $787 billion. Later, in February 2012 when most of the spending was completed, the Congressional Budget Office (CBO) estimated the Act would add about $831 billion to deficits from 2009 to 2019. In addition, the CBO stated that more than 90 percent of the stimulus's budgetary impact occurred by the end of 2011.[31] The table and graph below break down the estimated costs of the Recovery Act's major components.[32]

27 For a more comprehensive explanation of the Financial Crisis of 2008, visit http://baselinescenario.com/financial-crisis-for-beginners/.
28 "The Recovery Act," Recovery.gov, http://www.recovery.gov/About/Pages/The_Act.aspx.
29 For an introduction to Keynes and his major work, see Paul Krugman's introduction to Keynes's The General Theory, available at http://www.pkarchive.org/economy/GeneralTheoryKeynesIntro.html.
30 Greg Mankiw, "News Flash: Economists Agree," Greg Mankiw's Blog, http://gregmankiw.blogspot.com/2009/02/news-flash-economists-agree.html.
31 "Estimated Impact of the American Recovery and Reinvestment Act on Employment and Economic Output from October 2011 through December 2011," Congressional Budget Office, February 2012, http://www.cbo.gov/sites/default/files/cbofiles/attachments/02-22-ARRA.pdf.
32 "Breakdown of Funding," Recovery.gov, http://www.recovery.gov/Transparency/fundingoverview/Pages/fundingbreakdown.aspx.

BREAKDOWN OF FUNDS PAID OUT, BY CATEGORY (billions of dollars)

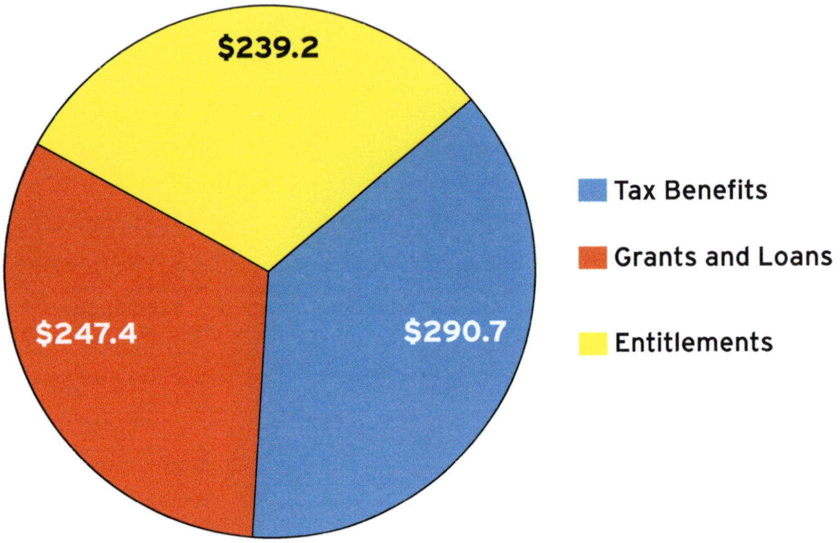

FIGURE 11

SOURCE: Recovery.gov, http://www.recovery.gov/Transparency/fundingoverview/Pages/fundingbreakdown.aspx.

TABLE 3 - BREAKDOWN OF FUNDS PAID OUT, BY CATEGORY

(billions of dollars)

Tax Benefits		Grants and Loans		Entitlements	
TOTAL	**$290.7**	**TOTAL**	**$247.4**	**TOTAL**	**$239.2**
Individual Tax Credits	$131.8	Education	$91.6	Medicaid/Medicare	$95.5
Making Work Pay	$104.4	Transportation	$36.7	Unemployment Insurance Programs	$61.1
Tax Incentives for Businesses	$32.6	Infrastructure	$30.7	Family Services	$44.9
Energy Incentives	$10.9	Energy/Environment	$28.2	Energy	$17.3
Manufacturing and Economic Recovery, Infrastructure Refinancing, Other	$7.3	R&D/Science	$14.3	Economic Recovery Payments	$13.8
COBRA	$3.7	Housing	$13.7	Housing	$5.6
		Health	$11.4	Agriculture	$1.0
		Other	$5.8		
		Public Safety	$5.3		
		Family	$5.0		
		Job Training/Unemployment	$4.7		

Tax cuts included temporary tax credits, additional tax exemptions, and tax incentives for hiring young and veteran workers. For example, the Act allotted $64.7 billion to temporarily increase the Alternative Minimum

Tax exemption, effectively decreasing tax rates on high incomes. The Act also instituted a temporary "Making Work Pay" tax credit to incentivize wage earning, which decreased revenues by $104.4 billion. In addition, the Act provided $1.2 billion in tax incentives for business investment in advanced energy facilities. Altogether, the stimulus provided nearly $300 billion in tax benefits, the largest component of the package.[33]

The grants and loans in the stimulus provided funds to maintain or increase spending on education, transportation, infrastructure, and other crucial functions of federal and state governments. In education, the Act provided states with nearly $50 billion to fund elementary and secondary education. In transportation, the Act gave an additional $25 billion to the Federal Highway Administration to invest in highway construction and improvements. Further, over $4.5 billion went to job training through the Department of Labor. Other grants went to programs in housing, research and development, energy, and public health, for a total of $236.4 billion in investments.[34]

Lastly, the Recovery Act expanded entitlements by $228.1 billion to assist families suffering decreased household income in the recession. For example, over $88 billion went to states to help them fund their Medicaid programs. The Act also expanded unemployment insurance by about $61 billion and the food stamp program by over $34 billion.[35]

THE RECOVERY ACT WORKED

A recent poll found that 80 percent of top economists across the ideological spectrum thought unemployment was lower at the end of 2010 than it would have been without the Recovery Act.[36] Further, several prominent analyses present evidence that the Recovery Act did indeed create jobs and stave off a deeper recession.

The CBO, often considered the definitive source for federal fiscal policy scoring, presented high and low estimates for the Recovery Act's effect on GDP and unemployment for every quarter from 2009 through 2013. Figures 12 and 13 below show the estimated impact in each quarter.[37]

As these figures show, the Recovery Act added to real GDP and reduced the unemployment rate every year since its passage and will likely continue to do so in 2013, compared to the CBO's counterfactual model of what the economy would have looked like without the stimulus.

Similarly, the President's Council of Economic Advisors found that the Act increased GDP by between 2.0 and 2.9 percent and raised employment by between 2.2 and 2.4 million jobs by the second quarter of 2011.[38]

Mark Zandi, chief economist at Moody's Analytics, put it simply: "The Recovery Act was passed in February of 2009, it began dispersing funds through tax cuts and spending increases soon thereafter, and by June of 2009, the recession was over. So it achieved its primary goal, which was to end the recession and jumpstart a recovery."[39]

33 "Tax Benefit Programs," Recovery.gov, http://www.recovery.gov/Transparency/fundingoverview/Pages/taxbenefits-details.aspx#IndividualTaxCredits.
34 "Contract, Grant and Loan Programs," Recovery.gov, http://www.recovery.gov/Transparency/fundingoverview/Pages/contractsgrantsloans-details.aspx#Education.
35 "Entitlement Programs," Recovery.gov, http://www.recovery.gov/Transparency/fundingoverview/Pages/entitlements-details.aspx#MedicaidMedicare.
36 "Economic Stimulus," IGM Forum, February 15, 2012, http://www.igmchicago.org/igm-economic-experts-panel/poll-results?SurveyID=SV_cw5O9LNJL1oz4Xi.
37 "Estimated Impact," 3.
38 "The Economic Impact of the American Recovery and Reinvestment Act of 2009, Eighth Quarterly Report," Council of Economic Advisors, December 9, 2009, http://www.whitehouse.gov/sites/default/files/cea_8th_arra_report_final_draft.pdf.
39 Mark Zandi, interview by author, June 19, 2012.

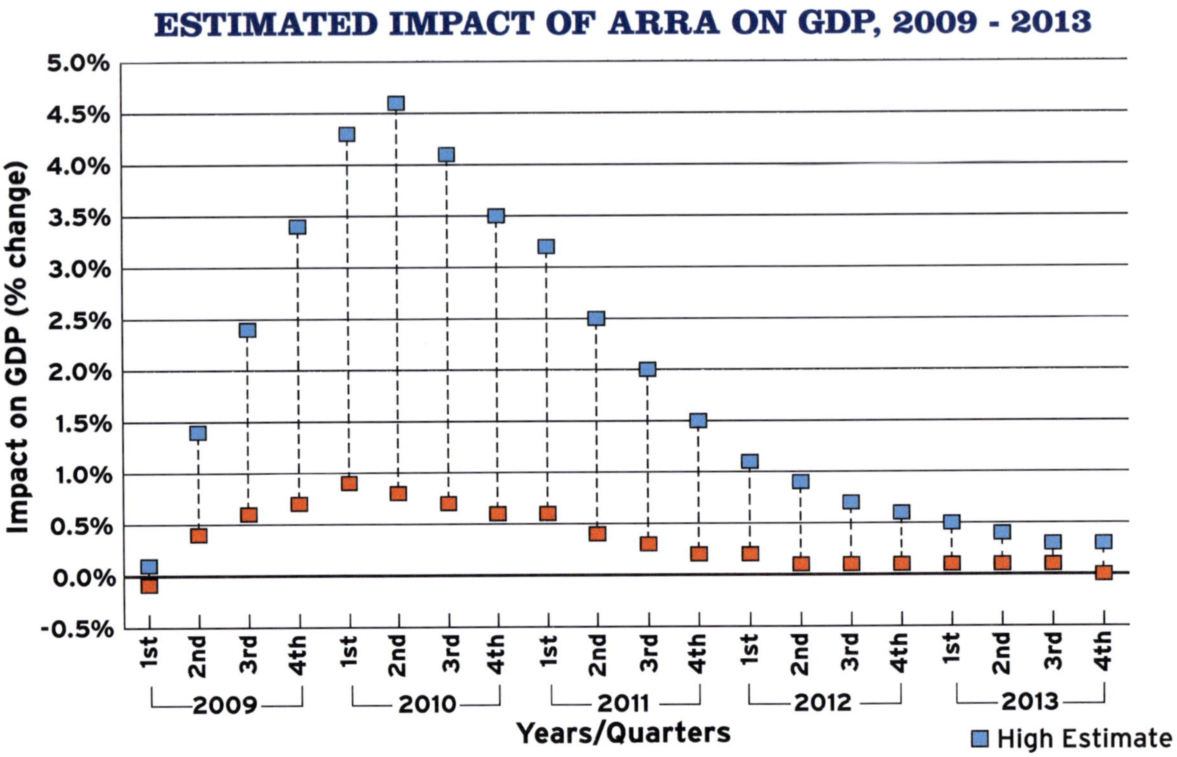

FIGURE 12

SOURCE: Congressional Budget Office, http://www.cbo.gov/sites/default/files/cbofiles/attachments/02-22-ARRA.pdf.

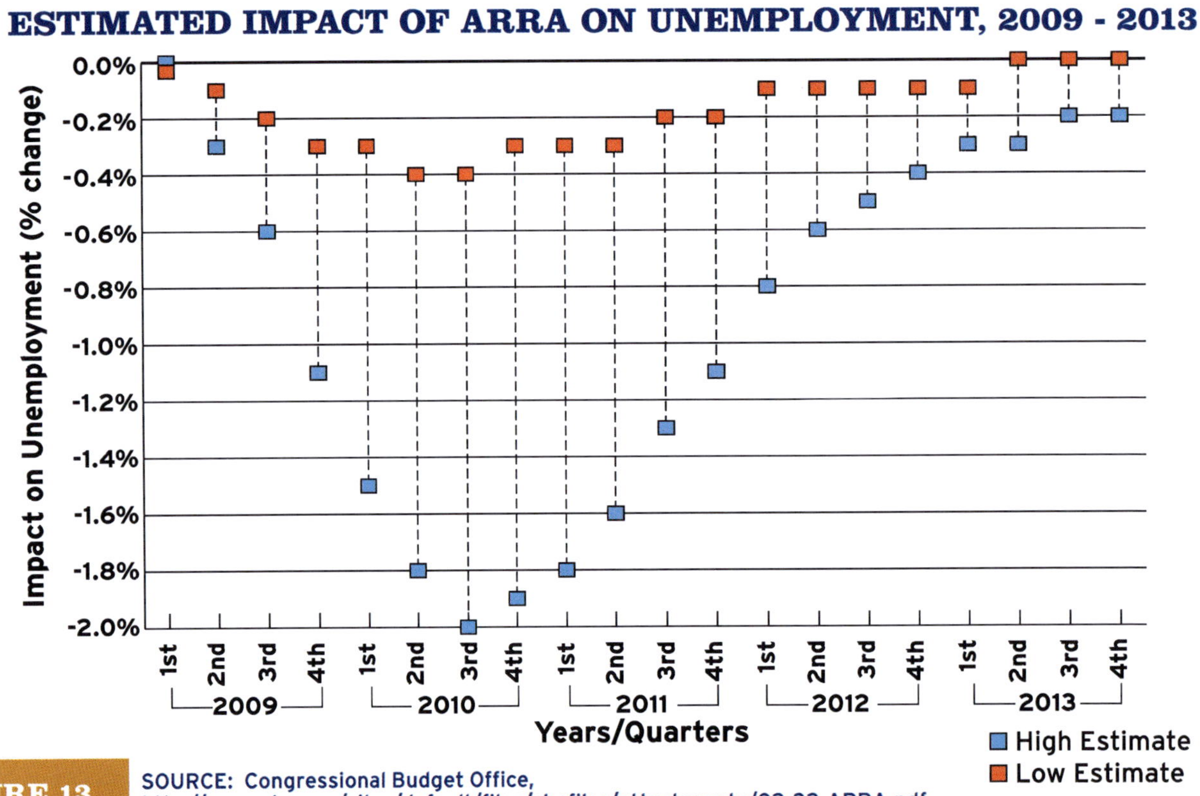

FIGURE 13

SOURCE: Congressional Budget Office, http://www.cbo.gov/sites/default/files/cbofiles/attachments/02-22-ARRA.pdf.

THE RECOVERY ACT DID NOT WORK

Other experts believe the Recovery Act did not achieve its goals.

Some economists dispute the idea that government spending can add to output, arguing instead that government spending predominately decreases spending and investment in the private sector. When the government borrows money, fewer funds are available in the market, and borrowers often must offer a higher interest rate to obtain a loan. Higher interest rates discourage businesses from investing and consumers from borrowing for large purchases. Economists call this "crowding out," and they argue that it reduces the efficacy of fiscal stimulus.

Stimulus proponents point to continued low interest rates due to the severity of the financial crisis as evidence that crowding out, in the Recovery Act's case, is not an issue. Opponents, however, insist that interest rates will rise in the future.

Harvard economist Robert Barro summed up much of the pro-stimulus position, which he opposes, nicely: "The theory (a simple Keynesian macroeconomic model) implicitly assumes that the government is better than the private market at marshaling idle resources to produce useful stuff." According to Barro and others, this assumption is faulty.[40]

Stanford economist John Taylor also criticized the Recovery Act, though for a different reason. He argued that the Act's main components—temporary tax cuts and transfers to state governments—were particularly ineffective methods of stimulus. The proportion of the package that went to direct government purchases and investments, he claimed, were "too small for the stimulus package to have had a significant effect on the overall economy."[41]

For one, Taylor argued that the temporary tax cuts and credits were largely saved rather than spent, causing a minimal stimulatory effect. To support his claim, he presented evidence that increases in disposable income from tax cuts in 2008 and 2009 had little noticeable affect on personal consumption.[42]

Taylor asserted that federal transfers to state governments, meant to prevent massive layoffs, tax increases, or spending cuts at the state and local level, were largely saved as well. Taylor noted, "States and local governments were adding significantly to their financial assets as ARRA grants came in. Indeed, it appears that they were saving the grant money rather than using it to increase expenditures."[43]

Harvard economist Martin Feldstein agreed with Taylor, writing, "It would have been better to have less of the money in transfers to states and others and more [in] sustained spending or spending stimulus."[44]

Public Opinion and The Future of Fiscal Stimulus

As previously noted, the Recovery Act added an estimated $831 billion to the national debt. Largely for that reason, the same survey that showed 80 percent of economists thought the stimulus helped the economy in 2010 was considerably less clear about the long-term merits of the Act. Asked whether, over the long-term, the "benefits

40 Robert J. Barro, "Government Spending Is No Free Lunch," *Wall Street Journal*, January 22, 2009, http://online.wsj.com/article/SB123258618204604599.html.
41 John B. Taylor, "An Empirical Analysis of the Revival of Fiscal Activism in the 2000s," *Journal of Economic Literature* 49, no. 3 (2011): 693.
42 Taylor, "Fiscal Activism," 690.
43 Taylor, "Fiscal Activism," 695.
44 Martin Feldstein, e-mail message to author, July 16, 2012.

of the stimulus will end up exceeding its costs," only 46 percent of economists agreed. Another 27 percent were uncertain, while 12 percent disagreed and 2 percent expressed no opinion.[45]

The American public also remains divided over the question, with 37 percent approving of Obama's 2009 stimulus plan, 41 percent disapproving, and 23 percent uncertain as of February 2012.[46]

TABLE 4 - PUBLIC OPINION OF FEBRUARY 2009 STIMULUS PLAN

	Approve	Disapprove	Don't Know
June 2009	55%	39%	6%
Sep 2009	44%	44%	12%
Feb 2010	38%	49%	13%
Feb 2012	37%	41%	23%

★

45 "Economic Stimulus."
46 "Auto Bailout Now Backed, Stimulus Divisive," Pew Research Center, February 23, 2012, http://www.people-press.org/2012/02/23/auto-bailout-now-backed-stimulus-divisive/.

RECOVERING FROM THE RECESSION: Quantitative Easing

by Rachel Wong

To combat the 2007 financial crisis, President Obama signed into law a massive stimulus package that cost an estimated $787 billion.[47] His rationale: pumping extra money into the economy would encourage Americans to buy more goods and services, which would boost commercial activity.

The Federal Reserve, America's central bank, has also been trying out new ways to fight the recession. The rationale is similar: pumping extra money into the economy helps our businesses. However, stimulus money from the Fed boosts the economy not by encouraging Americans to buy more from businesses but rather to invest more in them.

To understand how boosting investment helps out an economy, consider the following scenario. Imagine that John, who just graduated from high school, now wants to open a pizza parlor. Because he doesn't have the money on hand to rent a space and hire delivery boys, he first needs to take out a loan from his bank. He will pay the bank back when his business starts making money. As part of this loan agreement, John is charged an interest rate, or a percentage of the amount he borrowed. If the interest rate is low, then he does not have to pay the bank much more than the amount he borrowed, and it is easier for him to pay back his loan. As a result, low interest rates encourage borrowing to start businesses. This is good, because more investment is a sign of a healthy economy.

Two different scenarios—one with a high interest rate and one with a low interest rate—are illustrated in Table 5. As is clear from the bottom line, when John has a low interest rate, he does not have to pay the bank as much money in return for the loan, so it is easier for him to get rid of his debt. This makes taking a loan more attractive both for John and for the bank.

TABLE 5 - SCENARIO: LOANS FOR JOHN'S PIZZA PARLOR

	High Interest Rate – 10%	Low Interest Rate – 1%
Original Loan Amount	$10,000	$10,000
Loan Period	1 year	1 year
Interest Paid	$1,000	$100
Total Amount Repaid	**$11,000**	**$10,100**

In a recession, the Fed stimulates the economy by keeping interest rates low, which encourages investment. It normally achieves this by targeting a specific type of short-term interest rate called the federal funds rate, which applies to loans that banks make to each other. These funds are typically loaned out for short periods of time, often overnight. Lowering the federal funds rate makes it easier for banks to lend and borrow money, which boosts investment and makes it easier for people like John take out loans for their businesses.

A LIQUIDITY TRAP

In today's economy, however, the federal funds rate has already come very close to zero. This is known as a liquidity trap (Figure 14). Liquidity traps can occur when the Fed lowers the federal funds rate all the way to zero, but still cannot stimulate the economy enough. This is essentially what happened in 2009. As Chairman

47 "Obama: Stimulus Lets Americans Claim Destiny," MSNBC, February 17, 2009, http://www.msnbc.msn.com/id/29231790/ns/politics-white_house/t/obama-stimulus-lets-americans-claim-destiny/.

Bernanke observed a year later, the economy "has experienced periods of intense panic and dysfunction, during which private short-term funding became difficult or impossible to obtain for many borrowers."[48] Even with the federal funds rate near zero, the economy remained troubled.

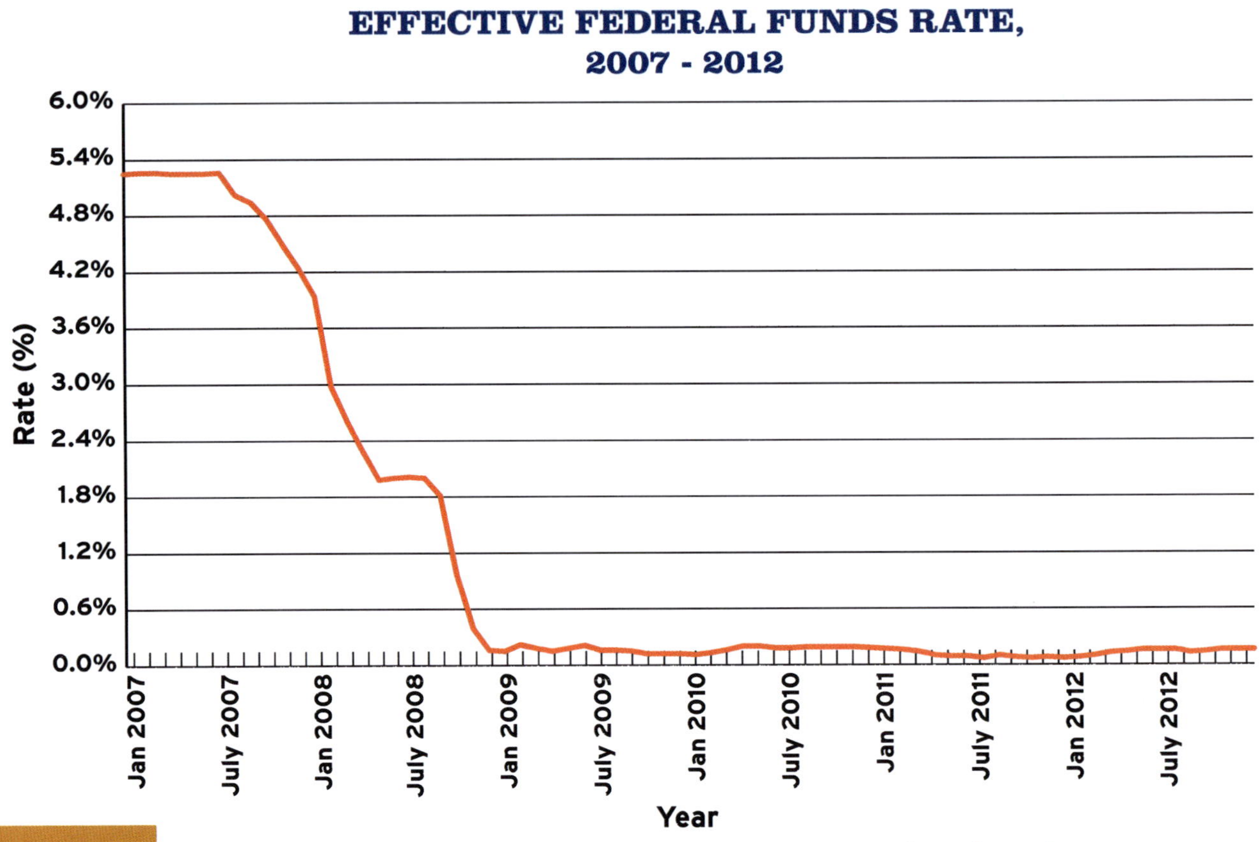

FIGURE 14 SOURCE: Federal Reserve Economic Data, http://research.stlouisfed.org/fred2/series/FEDFUNDS.

If the Fed cannot lower the federal funds rate any further, the Fed stimulates lending and borrowing through a new tool called quantitative easing (QE). As explained above, the federal funds rate applies to short-term, overnight loans between banks. Long-term interest rates follow the same trends as the federal funds rate, but since long-term loans may take years to pay back and are therefore riskier, interest rates are often set several percentage points higher (Figure 15). Even when the economy is in a liquidity trap, long-term interest rates may still be above zero. Quantitative easing tries to lower these rates, not the federal funds rate, so that the Fed can still promote investment and help stimulate an economy in recession. Faced with a near-zero federal funds rate after the 2008 financial crisis, Bernanke's Fed stepped into its first round of quantitative easing.

48 Ben Bernanke, "Federal Reserve's Exit Strategy," testimony before the Committee on Financial Services, U.S. House of Representatives, February 10, 2010, http://www.federalreserve.gov/newsevents/testimony/bernanke20100210a.htm.

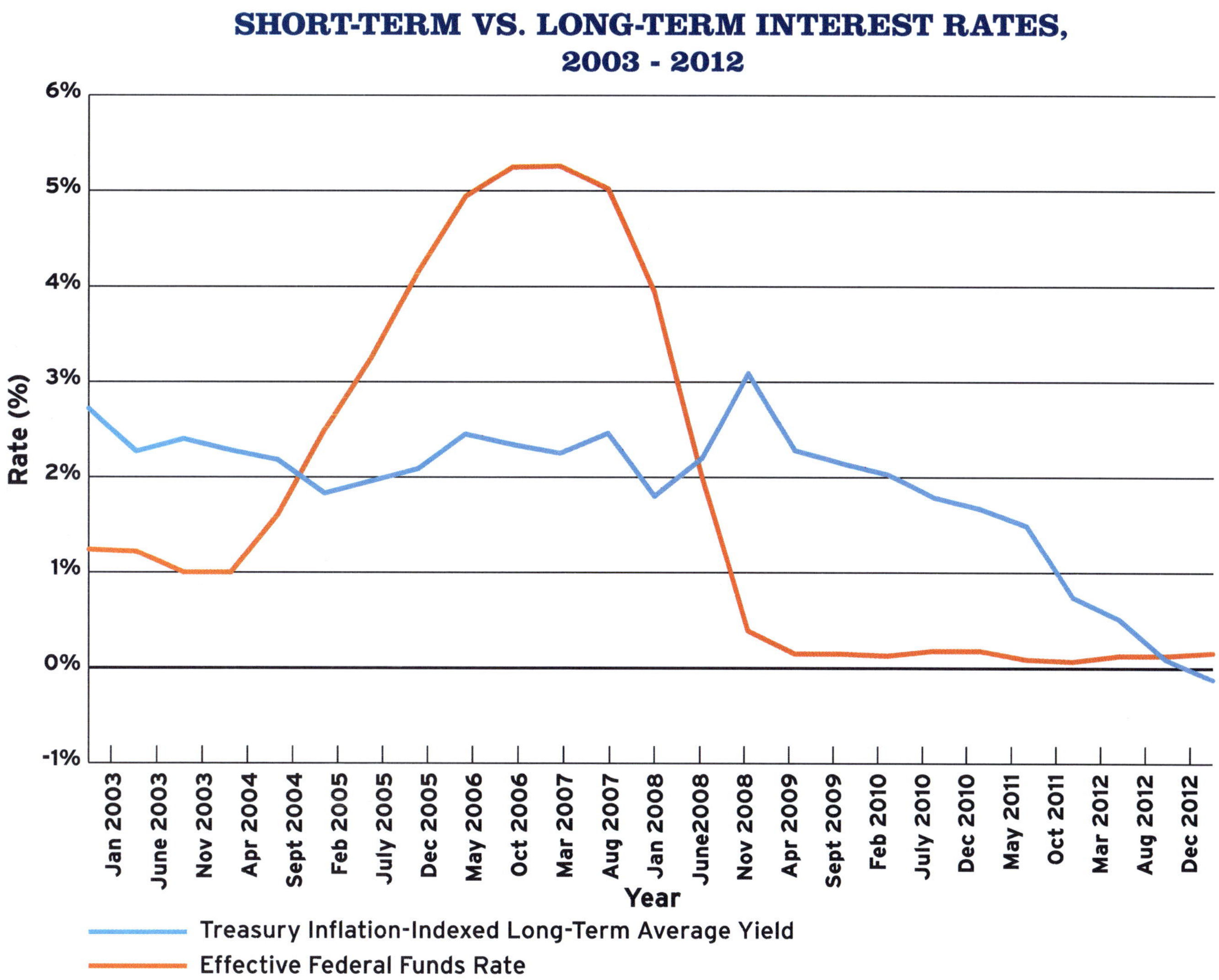

FIGURE 15 SOURCE: Federal Reserve Economic Data, http://research.stlouisfed.org/fred2/series/FEDFUNDS and http://research.stlouisfed.org/fred2/series/DLTIIT.

THE MECHANICS OF QUANTITATIVE EASING

At the peak of the financial crisis in 2008, the Fed began its QE efforts by buying large amounts of long-term debt, including Treasury securities (debt owed by the U.S. government) and mortgage-backed securities (debt owed by home buyers, abbreviated as MBS). The Fed's purchases reduced the supply of such Treasury securities and MBS in the market, and as they became scarcer, they also became more expensive. Following the economic rule relating price and interest rate for any security, as prices rose, interest rates fell. The Fed had accomplished its objective.

MORTGAGE-BACKED SECURITIES HELD BY THE FEDERAL RESERVE, 2007 - 2012

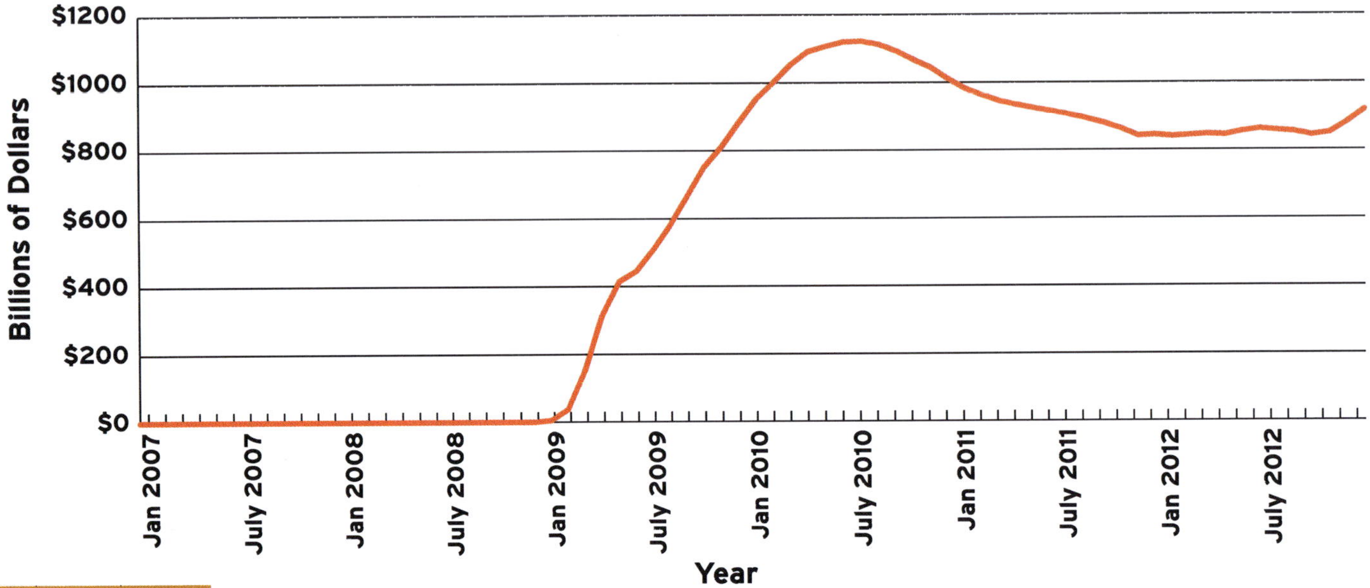

FIGURE 16 SOURCE: Federal Reserve Economic Data, http://research.stlouisfed.org/fred2/series/MBST.

Within the space of two months in late 2008, the Fed's assets expanded from $907 billion to $2.2 trillion. Because the Fed has the authority to create the money used to pay for these securities, this money enters directly into the banks' excess reserves, which are extra stores of money that banks hold with the Fed. Because of these large-scale asset purchases, excess reserves in banks rose from $2 billion to $767 billion in those two months.[49]

In late 2010, the Fed announced a second round of quantitative easing, QE2. To stimulate the still-sluggish economy, it pledged to buy $600 billion in Treasury securities in the coming year.[50] Whereas the Fed held a little over $700 billion in Treasuries before the recession, it now holds $1.7 trillion. The focus for QE2 was mainly on Treasury securities, but the Fed also committed to buying $32 billion in mortgage-backed securities within four months of the announcement. Its goal was to maintain its assets at a massive $2.054 trillion until the economy improved. Today, the Fed holds a total of $2.8 trillion in assets. This tremendous growth in assets demonstrates the importance of QE in the Fed's economic toolbox (Figure 16 and Table 6).

TABLE 6 - SELECTED ASSETS AND BANK RESERVES OF THE FED, BEFORE QE1 AND AFTER QE2

	Before QE1	After QE2
Total Assets	$869 billion	$2.8 trillion
Treasury Securities	$700 billion	$1.7 trillion
Mortgage-Backed Securities	$0	$1.25 trillion
Excess Bank Reserves	$2 billion	$1.45 trillion

49 Alan Blinder, "Quantitative Easing: Entrance and Exit Strategies," *Federal Reserve Bank of St. Louis Review* 92, no. 6 (November/December 2010), 469, http://research.stlouisfed.org/publications/review/10/11/Blinder.pdf.

50 James D. Hamilton and Jing Cynthia Wu, "The Effectiveness of Alternative Monetary Policy Tools in a Zero Lower Bound Environment," National Bureau of Economic Research, May 17, 2011, http://www.nber.org/papers/w16956.pdf.

RECOVERING FROM THE RECESSION: QUANTITATIVE EASING

REVIEW

The 2007 recession is different from past recessions in one important way: today, the federal funds rate is near zero, and our economy is in a liquidity trap.[51] This means that the Federal Reserve could not use its main weapon, lowering short-term interest rates, to help stimulate the economy. Instead, it had to use a new tool, quantitative easing, which was relatively untested and more than just a little risky, to lower long-term interest rates.

The first round of quantitative easing started in 2008, with massive purchases of Treasury securities and mortgage-backed securities. The Fed's total assets ballooned to $2.1 trillion as a result. With the economy still slow in 2010, a second round of quantitative easing, QE2, propelled holdings to $2.8 trillion. Most economists agree that QE has been at least moderately successful in lowering long-term interest rates.

The money created to pay for the Fed's spending spree has been deposited directly into excess bank reserves. If banks decide to lend this money out into the economy, the trillions of extra dollars could set off massive inflation. But at the moment, banks are willing to keep the money untouched—essentially, they are lending to the Fed until the economy recovers. That's why inflation has remained near normal levels.

There are two paths for the future of quantitative easing: QE could be the Fed's new long-term tool against future recessions, or it could simply be a risky and temporary fix that requires a careful exit. In 2010, the Fed announced that it would choose the latter path, outlining a strategy for draining the assets it acquired from QE.[52] Whether or not it really can implement a graceful exit remains to be seen, but one thing is certain: if Americans think the strategy is credible, then the Fed is more likely to succeed. Just as expectations shape inflation and long-term interest rates, the success (or failure) of the Fed's exit from quantitative easing will be in large part a self-fulfilling prophecy.

Experts on QE

Ben Bernanke, Chairman of the Federal Reserve: "Conditions in the banking system—and the financial sector more broadly—have improved significantly in the past few years."

Arvind Krishnamurthy and **Annette Vissing-Jorgensen**, Northwestern University: "We find a large and significant drop in nominal interest rates on medium and long-term safe assets."[53]

Alan Blinder, Princeton University: "The Fed's quantitative easing attack on interest rate spreads appears to have been successful, at least in part."[54]

James Hamilton, University of California, San Diego, and **Jing Cynthia Wu**, University of Chicago: "The potential small magnitude of the effect is not a concern as far as [quantitative easing] is concerned—

51 Even in the Great Depression, the federal funds rate never reached zero, hovering around 2 percent.

52 Ben Bernanke, "Federal Reserve's Exit Strategy," testimony before the Committee on Financial Services, U.S. House of Representatives, February 10, 2010, http://www.federalreserve.gov/newsevents/testimony/bernanke20100210a.htm.

53 Arvind Krishnamurthy and Annette Vissing-Jorgensen, "The Effects of Quantitative Easing on Interest Rates: Channels and Implications for Policy," National Bureau of Economic Research, October 2011, http://www.nber.org/papers/w17555.

54 Alan Blinder, "Quantitative Easing: Entrance and Exit Strategies," *Federal Reserve Bank of St. Louis Review* 92, no. 6 (November/December 2010): 465-79.

if hundreds of billions are not enough to make much difference, then perhaps purchases in the trillions, such as the Fed has embarked upon with its holdings of mortgage-backed securities, might do the trick."[55]

Can Expectations Shape QE?

Speculation about quantitative easing may affect expectations of future interest rates, thereby influencing market behavior. As Brookings Institution Senior Fellow Justin Wolfers explained, "If the Fed says 'we want long-run interest low and we have a big pile of money right here that we are going to use to do that,' they ultimately don't have to use the money because the markets understand that they could always use that money if needed, and so long-run interest rates fall very quickly."

Whether the drop in interest rates is due to QE2, or to investors' expectations, it is likely that the Fed's aggressive policy has helped stimulate the economy, at least for the time being.

Scenario, Part II: John's Pizza Parlor and the Future of QE

John: It seems like the two rounds of quantitative easing have been moderately effective. How does that help me set up my pizza place?

The Fed: Remember that the goal of QE is to lower long-term interest rates, even when the shorter-term federal funds rate can't fall any further. This makes it easier for you to borrow the money you need to start your business. Lower interest rates mean you won't need to pay back as much on your loan.

John: Great, it sounds like the Fed is helping me save money! But the entire QE program is costing trillions of dollars. Who's paying for all this?

The Fed: The short answer is that we are creating this money from scratch. Rather than printing money, we are expanding credit: payment for assets is deposited at banks in the form of excess reserves. In other words, we are crediting banks with digital money for all the Treasury securities and MBS that we bought.

John: What's the long answer?

The Fed: Economists disagree over the long-term costs of QE. Some argue that we are trying to stimulate the economy by "transferring immense wealth from the middle-class to the most affluent, from the least privileged to the most privileged."[56] People preparing for retirement may find themselves losing their savings, since they are earning much less interest on their deposits at the bank. Borrowers like you may be happy to get loans at low rates, but savers ultimately lose out.

Others believe that QE helps the general population, not the privileged few: "I know the picture: retirees living on the interest on their bank account and their fixed pension check," wrote Paul Krugman, "and there are no doubt some people fitting that description. But there aren't many of them."[57] In fact, Krugman

55 James D. Hamilton and Jing Cynthia Wu, "The Effectiveness of Alternative Monetary Policy Tools in a Zero Lower Bound Environment," National Bureau of Economic Research, May 17, 2011, http://www.nber.org/papers/w16956.pdf.
56 Mark Spitznagel, "How the Fed Favors the 1%," *Wall Street Journal*, April 19, 2012, http://online.wsj.com/article/SB10001424052702304356604577343430113336486.html.
57 Paul Krugman, "Plutocrats and Printing Presses," *The New York Times*, April 20, 2012, http://krugman.blogs.nytimes.com/2012/04/20/plutocrats-and-printing-presses/.

argued, QE hurts banks most, since they make money by borrowing on short-term interest rates and lending out at long-term rates.

John: Wait a minute. Isn't it dangerous for the Fed just to make trillions of dollars out of thin air?

The Fed: It is risky, to say the least. If this money were suddenly released into the economy, the influx of extra dollar bills would set off inflation—each dollar within the U.S. economy would be worth much less, since there would be so many more of them floating around.

As often stated by economists, "too many dollars chasing too few goods" will cause prices to rise, making it harder for Americans to pay their bills. Just take a look at the numbers: As of May 2012, total currency circulating in the economy was $1.1 trillion, whereas the total number of dollars in excess bank reserves was $1.45 trillion. If these excess reserves flooded the economy at once, prices would skyrocket.

John: But if creating money causes inflation, then why aren't prices rising now?

The Fed: At the moment, inflation is low, hovering around 2 percent. This is because banks are happy to let the funds from QE stay in their excess reserves, at least for the time being. Even though lending out these reserves to borrowers like you would earn the banks income on the interest rates they would charge, lending out all of this extra money at once would set off disastrous inflation. We are actually paying banks to keep their reserves untouched. At the moment, they don't mind doing so. The economy is still a bit too risky for them to loan out that much money anyway.

Figure 17 below shows that the total number of dollars in the economy has remained relatively stable over the past few years, while excess reserves have increased dramatically.

CURRENCY IN CIRCULATION AND EXCESS RESERVES, 2006 - 2012

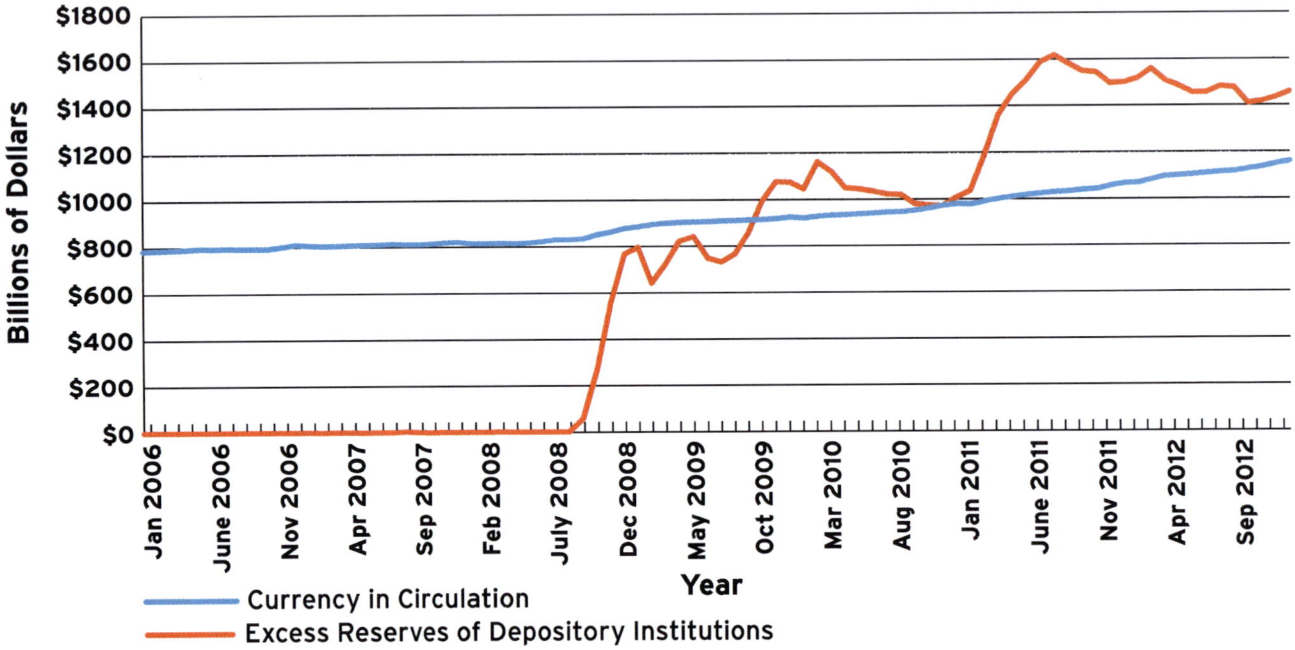

FIGURE 17

SOURCE: Federal Reserve Economic Data, http://research.stlouisfed.org/fred2/series/CURRCIR and http://research.stlouisfed.org/fred2/series/EXCRESNS.

John: So how do we get out?

The Fed: We have several strategies for draining banks' excess reserves without flooding the economy with extra money. Together this package is known as the exit strategy. It includes selling off the securities we bought and raising the interest rates that we pay for excess reserves. But not everyone agrees that an "exit" is really necessary. Harvard economist Benjamin Friedman believes that we could also use QE much like we use the federal funds rate—as a powerful tool for controlling the economy.[58]

John: What does this exit strategy have to do with me?

The Fed: If Americans don't believe that we can deal with the risks of QE, then they will expect massive inflation in the future. This is a self-fulfilling prophecy: high inflation expectations cause business owners to raise prices now. The rise in prices makes the dollar worth less, which causes high inflation, just as expected. Therefore, it is critical that Americans feel confident that the Fed can handle the consequences of QE. For example, William Dudley, President of the Federal Reserve Bank of New York, believes that the Fed "should be able to assure investors that it has both the means and the will to exit when—but not before—the time is right."[59]

★

58 Benjamin Friedman, interview by author, June 12, 2012.
59 William C. Dudley, "The Outlook, Policy Choices and Our Mandate," Federal Reserve Bank of New York, October 1, 2010, http://www.newyorkfed.org/newsevents/speeches/2010/dud101001.html.

ENTITLEMENT SPENDING: Social Security

by John Kocsis

The term "Social Security" actually refers to a collection of federal welfare programs that began in 1935 as Old-Age, Survivors, and Disability Insurance. OASDI itself comprises two separate programs: Old-Age and Survivors Insurance (OASI) and Disability Insurance (DI). Together, they are known as OASDI, the New Deal initiative enacted to help the elderly and the disabled during the Great Depression. Social Security is thus primarily a social insurance system for retirees.

The Social Security Trust Fund is the distinguishing characteristic of Social Security, and it is responsible for footing what many view as a bill that cannot be paid. Like the majority of government programs, its funding derives from taxes. However, Social Security and Medicare are unique in that their financing does not come from income taxes. They are paid through obligations from Federal Insurance Contributions Act (FICA) taxes, which are directly collected from workers' paychecks. This makes FICA a "payroll tax." The burden of this duty is split between the employer and the employee. In previous years, this amount was designated at 6.2 percent for each payer. In 2010, the employee share was lowered to 4.2 percent in a temporary tax reduction, but the payroll tax holiday ended in January 2013 with the American Taxpayer Relief Act of 2012. Today, the employee contribution is again at 6.2 percent. This year, the maximum income taxable under FICA is $110,100, a 3.1 percent increase from last year. In other words, no matter how much each earner made, no employee is expected to contribute more than $6,826.20 annually, and no employer is expected to contribute more than this amount for any employee.[60]

SOCIAL SECURITY SPENDING, 1962 - 2012 (real)

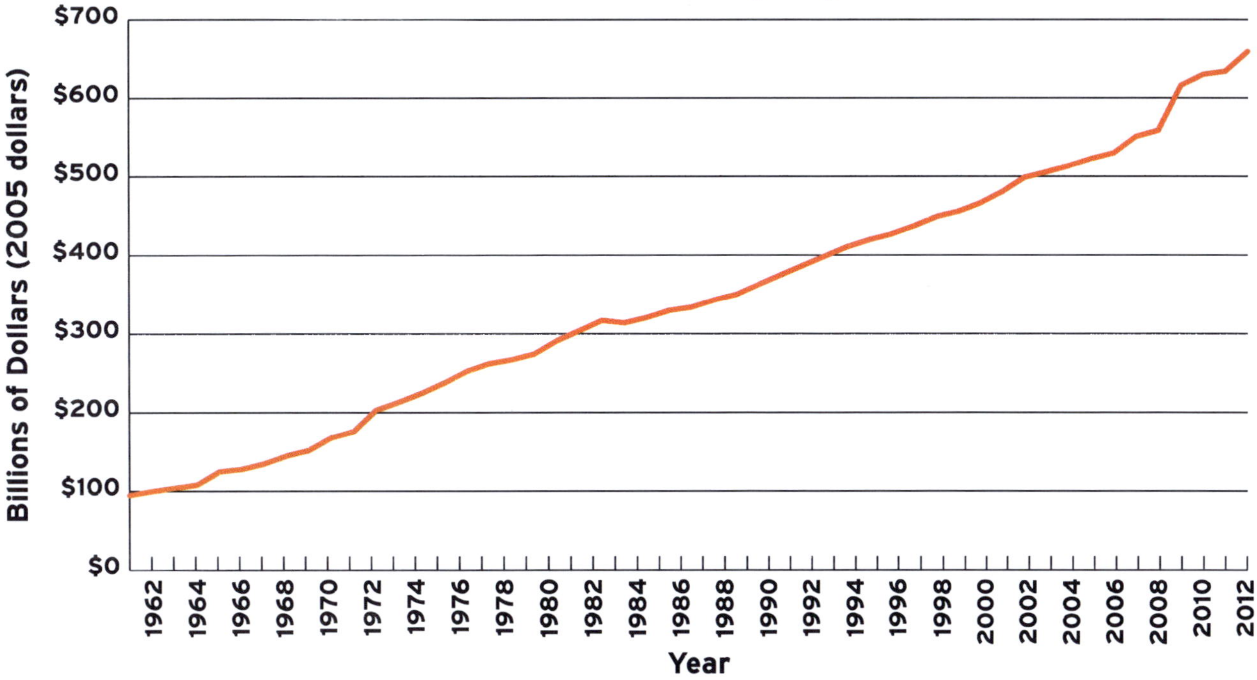

FIGURE 18 SOURCE: Budget of the U.S. Government FY 2013, http://www.gpo.gov/fdsys/pkg/BUDGET-2013-TAB/xls/BUDGET-2013-TAB-3-2.xls.

60 "Social Security Taxable Wage Limit and Employee Rate Increased For Year 2012," ADP Tax Researcher 28 (November 2011): 11.

ENTITLEMENT SPENDING: SOCIAL SECURITY

THE NUMBERS

TABLE 7 - SOCIAL SECURITY SPENDING millions of dollars			
	2011	2012	2013
Discretionary Spending	$5,638	$5,738	$5,767
Old-age and Survivors Insurance	$597,780	$637,360	$680,453
Disability Insurance	$128,396	$138,071	$143,896
Accounting policies	-$84	$3	$203
Total Spending	**$731,730**	**$781,172**	**$830,319**

While the Social Security Trust Fund is currently well afloat, if structural changes are not made, it will become weighed down by an outsize anchor of liabilities far exceeding its own weight.[61]

Discretionary spending is not continuously mandated by federal law. Instead, this spending is determined for a single year through the annual appropriations process in Congress. The administrative costs that facilitate the operation of the Social Security Administration are part of discretionary spending.

The Social Security benefits, OASI and DI, are paid for through mandatory spending, meaning that their yearly allocation is predetermined by federal law.

The federal government reconciles the amount spent on programs through various accounting measures enabled by intergovernmental transactions. The amount was negative in 2011 due to an adjustment every five years that revalues military wage credits.

TRUST FUND RESULTS AND COMPOSITION, FY 2011 (billions of dollars)

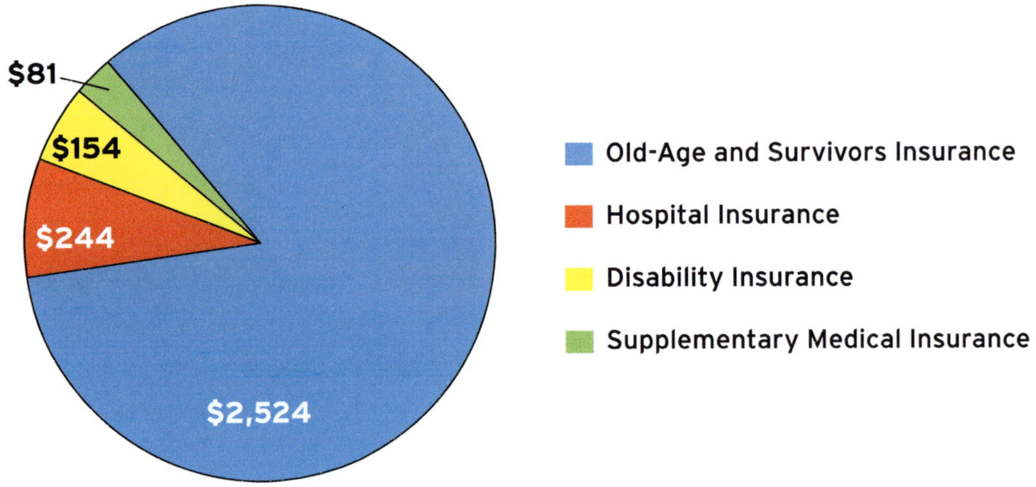

FIGURE 19 SOURCE: Social Security and Medicare Boards of Trustees, http://www.ssa.gov/oact/trsum/index.html.

61 Data from Office of Management and Budget, 2012.

ANALYSIS

TABLE 8 - KEY DATES FOR THE TRUST FUNDS			
	OASI	DI	OASDI
Year of peak trust fund ratio	2011	2003	2011
First year outgo exceeds income excluding interest	2010	2005	2010
First year outgo exceeds income including interest	2023	2009	2021
Year trust funds are exhausted	2035	2016	2033

SOURCE: "A Summary of the 2012 Annual Reports," Social Security and Medicare Boards of Trustees, http://www.ssa.gov/OACT/TRSUM/index.html.

At first glance, the numbers are no so intimidating. After all, the $781 billion in benefits can easily be covered by the $2.6 trillion in assets held by the Social Security Trust Fund. The picture becomes less rosy, however, when an important fact is added: SSA only collected $564 billion in payroll tax receipts in 2011, a number that is expected to decline sharply as more people retire from the work force.

COVERED WORKERS PER OASDI BENEFICIARY, 1960 - 2090

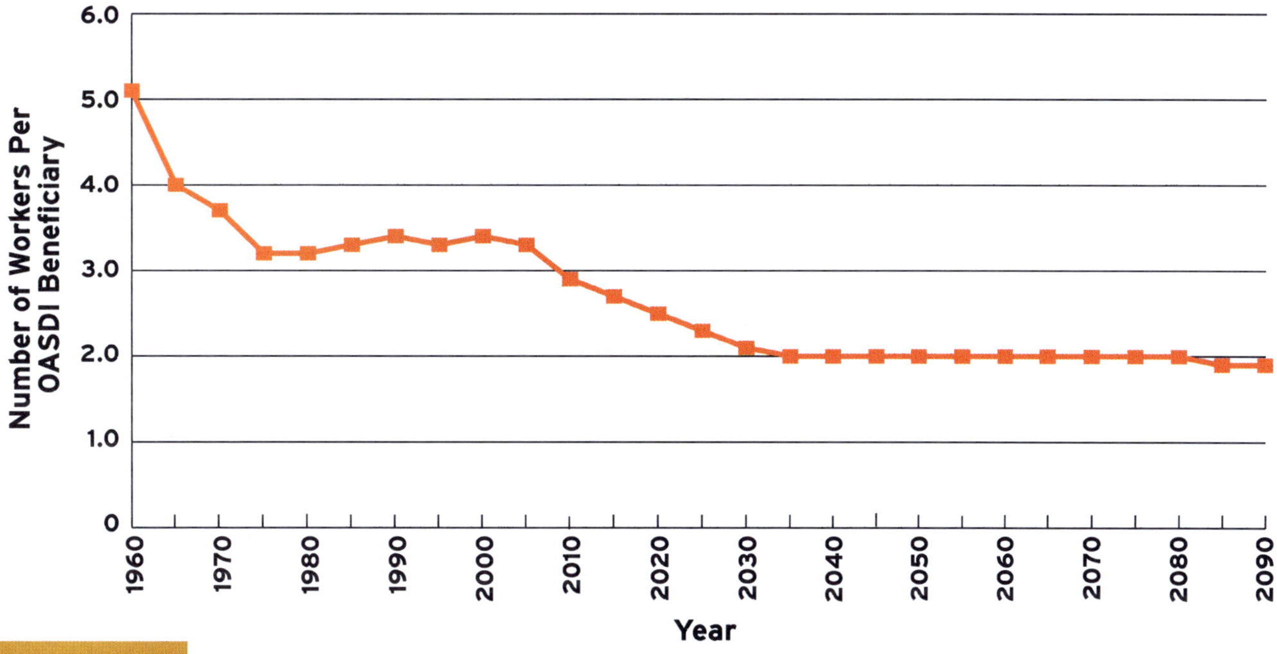

FIGURE 20 SOURCE: Social Security Administration, http://www.ssa.gov/oact/tr/2012/IV_B_LRest.html.

In other words, the current revenue-benefit system is unsustainable to some degree. In their Annual Report, the Trustees of the Social Security Trust Fund admitted that the fund is projected to run out in 2033—three years earlier than what had been previously expected. However, they presented their analysis in optimistic terms, claiming that the funds will continue to grow until at least 2020.[62]

62 2012 Annual Report, The Board of Trustees of the Federal Old-Age And Survivors Insurance and Federal Disability Insurance Trust Funds, April 25, 2012, http://www.ssa.gov/oact/tr/2012/trTOC.html.

While it is universally recognized that the current fund will not last forever (or even very far into the future), the implications of this fact are the subject of much debate. This has sparked a divide between those on the Right and on the Left, which can be partly explained by a fundamental disagreement over what the Social Security Trust Fund actually is.

Unlike private trust funds, the Social Security Trust Fund does not retain the revenue it collects from those who pay into the system. When money is raised from employers and employees who pay FICA taxes, it is immediately used to pay the country's retirees, the beneficiaries of the program. The government then uses any excess revenues to pay for other budgetary programs. This creates some interesting technicalities, since the verbiage of payroll tax legislation specifically ties it to a benefit. The Social Security Act explicitly created a "Social Security tax" to pay for retirees' Social Security, neglecting to allow that money to be spent on other endeavors. To compensate for the fact that these Social Security taxes are actually used for other discretionary programs, the Trust Fund trades the revenue for United States Treasury bonds. While these bonds are not actual currency, they accrue interest until their maturation date. At that point, the Treasury repays the value of the bond with interest. Since this amount is more than what the Trust Fund originally gave the federal government, this results in an increase in revenue.

> **"In other words, they say that if you write yourself IOUs, you have created wealth." –Michael Tanner, Cato Institute**

This complex operation leads to debates about the ambiguity embedded in Social Security's nature. Thought leaders on the Right view the fund as an accounting gimmick, since a portion of its assets comes from one arm of the government giving money to another arm of the government. They argue that paying for Social Security with manufactured money is unsustainable.

A LABOR PROBLEM?

> **"But ultimately, in the short term the main problem is high unemployment and a low rate of growth." –Greg Anrig, Century Foundation**
>
> **"Social Security is not running out of money. It currently maintains a 5 percent deficit, which is really reflective of a poor labor market." –Christian Weller, Center for American Progress**

Liberal thinkers disagree with this "alarmist" characterization. They protest that the wealth the Trust Fund accumulates from government bonds is exactly the same as wealth accrued by anyone who invests in Treasury bonds. While Social Security has entered a period in which its outflow exceeds its income, the $2.6 trillion interest payments mitigate this problem by covering the gap in what is owed.

Progressives believe that reforming a program that does not contribute to the national debt would be unproductive, and they instead seek a closer examination of the societal problems at the heart of Social Security's insecurity. While conservative and libertarian thinkers direct most of the conversation to the increasingly perilous demographic trends leading to insolvency, liberals blame larger economic problems; Democrats argue that the program would not appear to be in such dire straits if the country were not facing a weak economy that limits the scale of tax receipts.

> **"[The paralysis] is simply to provide the groundwork for an eventual destruction of Social Security, naturally in the name of 'saving it.' Which is to underline the strictly political character of the debate." –Richard M. Adams, University of California, Berkeley**

While different voices in the Social Security debate vary in their perspectives on the crisis, many believe there is a political element to the scenario and think back to earlier times. While the previous two presidents—one Republican, one Democrat—both flirted with privatization, such a plan is now toxic to Democrats and Republicans in blue states.[63] This new reality has changed the landscape of the debate, another manifestation of polarization in Washington, D.C. Leaders on both sides of the aisle lament this, recognizing the slim chance of any sort of compromise. Most Republicans will only consider privatization; Democrats, anything but. While both political parties make the claim Social Security is an issue that should be addressed, neither echoes the urgency of its words with actions.

TABLE 9 - SOCIAL SECURITY: ANOTHER LEFT-RIGHT DIVIDE

Progressive Priorities	Conservative Priorities
Concentrate on fixing economy	Set up private accounts
Reform benefit distribution	Invest in financial markets, which are steady in the long run
Fix survivor benefits (i.e., benefits for spouses)	Establish ownership of real capital assets
Reconsider earnings cap	Allow current beneficiaries to keep program

Regardless of political affiliation, everyone acknowledges that, at some point, certain components of Social Security need to be addressed if total system collapse is to be avoided. The Trustees' Report itself noted the need for eventual change, citing recommendations for potential revenue increases or benefit reductions. The report indicated that if lawmakers wait until 2033 to make changes to the program, they would then need to raise payroll taxes to 16.7 percent, followed by continual tax increases until 2086. Alternatively, the report proposed reduction of benefits by 25 percent in 2033 and continued reduction until 2086.[64]

THE IMPORTANCE OF THE SOCIAL SECURITY DISCUSSION

Social Security is currently solvent, and, as the data show, obligations are being met. Retirees are receiving their benefits. But liberals and conservatives alike admit there is some measure of danger in letting the current state of Social Security continue. This should be important to all voters—elderly voters because they may find themselves losing benefits they currently receive; middle-aged voters because they may receive significantly less than their parents do; and younger voters because they may never receive anything at all.

63 Angie Drobnic Holan and Lukas Pleva, "Democratic Exaggerations about 'Privatizing Social Security,'" PolitiFact, September 2, 2010, http://www.politifact.com/truth-o-meter/article/2010/sep/02/democratic-exaggerations-about-privatizing-social-/.

64 2012 Annual Report, The Board of Trustees of the Federal Old-Age And Survivors Insurance and Federal Disability Insurance Trust Funds, April 25, 2012, http://www.ssa.gov/oact/tr/2012/trTOC.html.

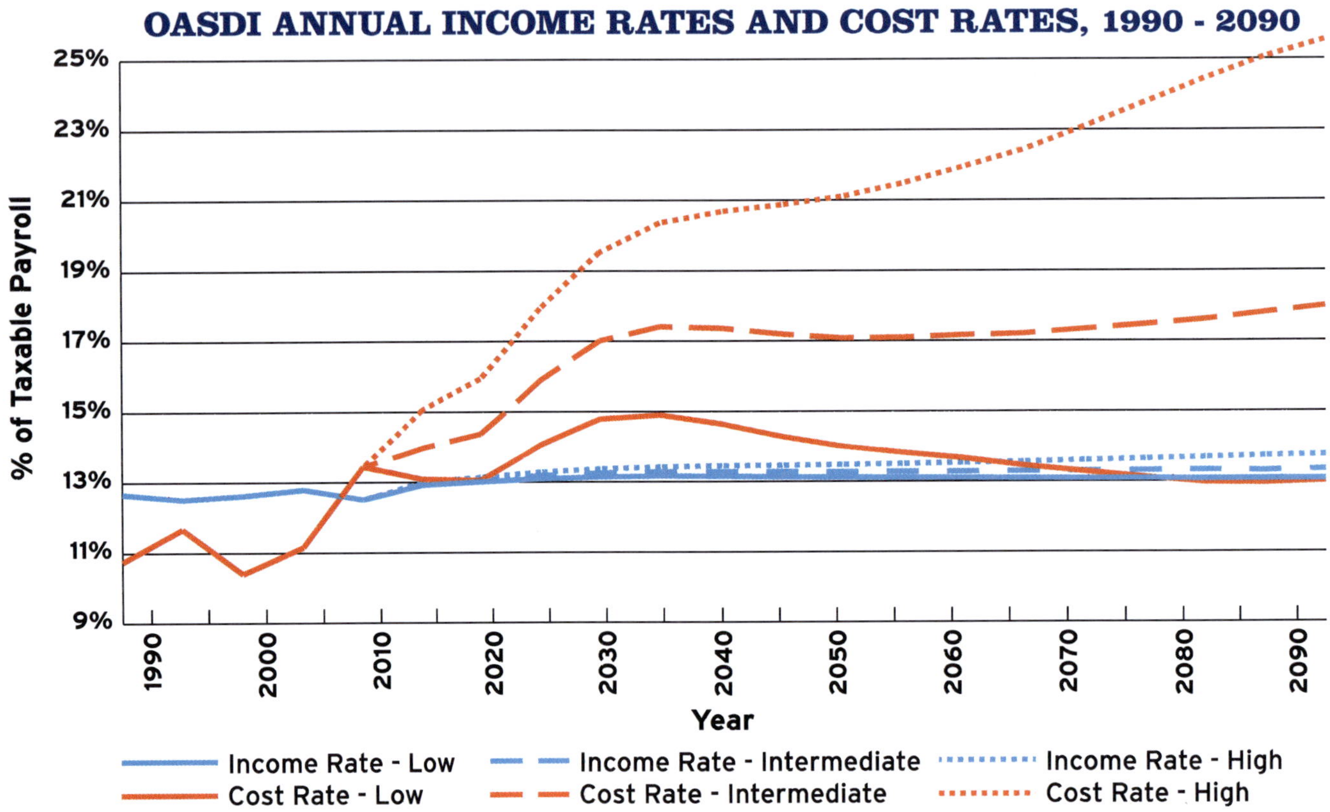

FIGURE 21 SOURCE: Social Security Administration, http://www.ssa.gov/oact/tr/2012/IV_B_LRest.html.

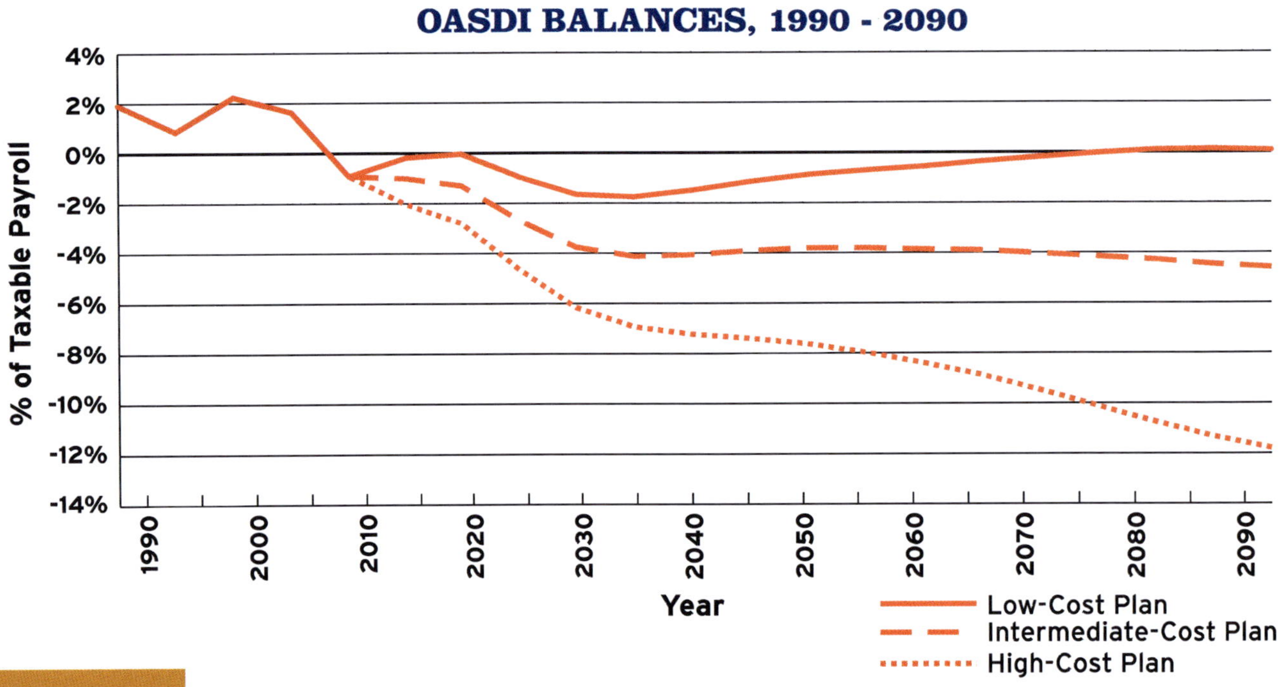

FIGURE 22 SOURCE: Social Security Administration, http://www.ssa.gov/oact/tr/2012/IV_B_LRest.html.

★

ENTITLEMENT SPENDING: HEALTH CARE

by Divya Seth

The U.S. health care system is intricately intertwined with the health insurance system. Health insurance is a treaty of sorts, reconciling the needs of individuals with the demands of the system. Individuals agree to pay premiums, and health insurance providers agree that they will foot a portion of the bill for a medical visit. While the insurer may cover a portion of the cost, the individual will likely pay a co-payment or be required to pay a deductible, which are defined as out-of-pocket expenses. Health insurance providers gamble that they will earn more from collecting premiums than from covering medical visit costs. And individuals, in the existing medical market, rely on health insurance to make good health care affordable.[65]

Definitions:

Jargon	Explanation
Deductible	The amount that an individual must pay for services before an insurance company will begin to reimburse health care costs.
Premium	A sum that a person must pay periodically for insurance coverage.
Fee for Service	A system that charges health care on a service-by-service basis.
Individual Mandate	Requirement to purchase health care, with a penalty tax on individuals who can purchase health insurance but choose not to.
High-Risk Insurance Pool	Insurance groups set up by states for those who do not have access to employer-based health insurance.
Bundled Payments	A system that charges health care based on a continuum of care.

In 2005, 80 percent of Americans purchased health insurance through their employers. Known as group health insurance, this option is preferred because it allows employers to purchase insurance plans at lower premiums for their employees than employees could purchase individually. In contrast, individual health insurance premiums are more expensive but provide a good option for those who are not covered or not covered enough by their employer.

Other than private insurance options, the government also provides two primary insurance options for some Americans. Medicare serves people over 65 years old, those with certain disabilities, and people with end-stage renal disease. Medicaid is available for low-income individuals and families that also fit specific requirements mandated by the government.

The basic model for most insurance plans is known as the fee-for-service (FFS) model. This system provides basic coverage for a range of medical costs, such as office visits, inpatient care, and surgeries, in exchange for a deductible, which is the amount that patients must pay before they can be reimbursed for health care costs by their insurers.

Managed care, such as a health maintenance organization (HMO), is a variant of FFS insurance, with the major difference being that these plans operate within pre-selected networks of doctors, hospitals, and clinics.

65 Lee Ann Obringer and Melissa Jeffries, "Understanding Health Insurance," How Stuff Works, February 4, 2006, http://tlc.howstuffworks.com/family/health-insurance.htm.

There are numerous variations and combinations of these two basic model types, creating a myriad of health insurance options.[66]

FEDERAL SPENDING ON HEALTH CARE, 1962 - 2012 (real)

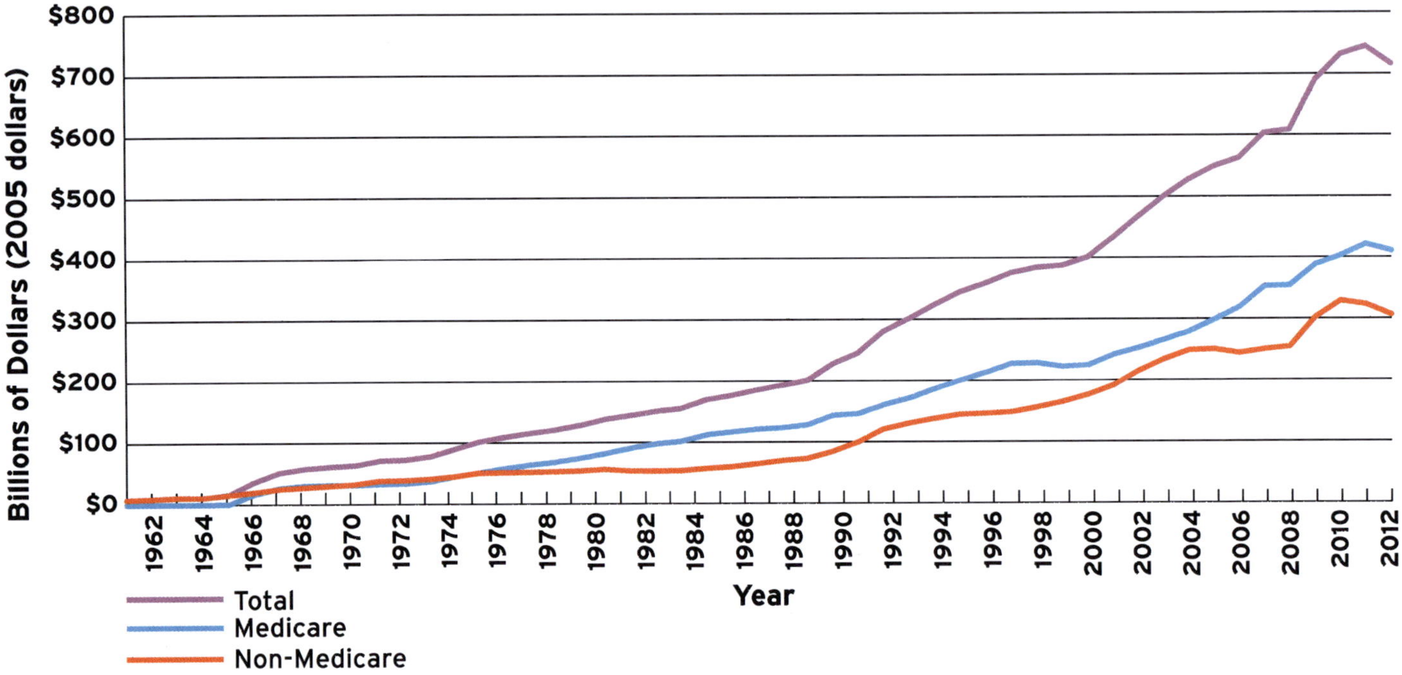

FIGURE 23

SOURCE: Budget of the U.S. Government FY 2013, http://www.gpo.gov/fdsys/pkg/BUDGET-2013-TAB/xls/BUDGET-2013-TAB-3-2.xls.

THE PROBLEM OF HEALTH CARE COVERAGE

In 2010, the U.S. Census Bureau reported, 49.9 million Americans did not have health insurance.[67] Research by the Urban Institute, a non-partisan economic and social policy research center, showed that the people are uninsured mostly due to the high costs of medical insurance.[68] According to the Robert Wood Johnson Foundation, from 2001 to 2005, income increased by 3.0 percent while health insurance costs rose 30 percent.[69] In 2008, the total annual premium for a typical family health insurance plan, as offered by employers, was $12,680.[70] To put that into perspective, the average household income in Mississippi in 2008 was $37,790.[71] A widely cited and controversial paper in *Health Affairs* noted that nearly 54 percent of personal bankruptcies were attributable to health care costs.[72] It is statistics like these that provided the momentum for a government-led reform of the American health care system.

66 Lee Ann Obringer and Melissa Jeffries, "Understanding Health Insurance," How Stuff Works, February 4, 2006, http://tlc.howstuffworks.com/family/health-insurance.htm.
67 "Health Insurance: Highlights, 2010," U.S. Census Bureau, September 14, 2011, http://www.census.gov/hhes/www/hlthins/data/incpovhlth/2010/highlights.html.
68 John Graves and Sharon K. Long, "Why Do People Lack Health Insurance?" Urban Institute, May 22, 2006, http://www.urban.org/publications/411317.html.
69 "Cost of Insurance Far Outpaces Income," Robert Wood Johnson Foundation, April 29, 2008, http://www.rwjf.org/healthpolicy/product.jsp?id=28698.
70 "Employer Health Benefits: 2008 Summary of Findings," Kaiser Family Foundation, 2008, http://ehbs.kff.org/images/abstract/7791.pdf.
71 Jessica Semega, "Median Household Income for States: 2007 and 2008 American Community Surveys," U.S. Census Bureau, September 2009, http://www.census.gov/prod/2009pubs/acsbr08-2.pdf.
72 David Himmelstein, et al., "Illness and Injury as Contributors to Bankruptcy," *Health Affairs* (2005), http://content.healthaffairs.org/content/early/2005/02/02/hlthaff.w5.63.full.pdf+html.

Health insurance in America is relatively new, and it has changed substantially in a short period of time. As late as 1920, while the European nations were adopting various forms of state-run health care coverage, there was still almost no market for health insurance, then known as "sickness" insurance, in the U.S. However, from 1920 to 1930, as demands for improved health care increased, the costs of health care began to rise, precipitating the formation of pre-paid hospital service plans in Dallas, Texas. During the Great Depression, these plans thrived, and health insurance giants Blue Cross and Blue Shield were created. From 1940 to 1960, the nation saw a huge growth in the health insurance market, with enrollment jumping from around 20 million in 1940 to more than 140 million in 1950. The 1960s were a time of great debate on the creation of a government-operated health care system, a debate that led to the formation of Medicare and Medicaid. More recently, in 2006, Massachusetts implemented health care reform, creating more affordable plans and expanding public programs for those without employer-sponsored insurance.[73]

The Affordable Care Act

The most recent and notable event in American health care history was the passage of the Patient Protection and Affordable Care Act, which was signed into law by President Obama on March 23, 2010. The Supreme Court upheld PPACA as constitutional in a set of rulings on June 28, 2012, with the caveat that the individual mandate will be a tax on individuals who do not purchase health care insurance.[74]

To understand the health care reform debate, it is important to first grasp the basic provisions of PPACA. Although the legislation fills over 900 pages, its premise is simple: improve health care access for all Americans and manage health care costs while controlling the nation's deficit.

PPACA aims to expand health care and health insurance access through various reforms that are designed to go into effect gradually over the coming years. The first of these steps addresses changes in private health insurance and puts forth new requirements in order to expand insurance coverage and prevent individuals from losing coverage. This has already been put into effect: young adults are now covered on their parents' insurance plans until they are 26 years old, health care insurance cannot be denied to an individual based on pre-existing conditions, and there are no dollar limits on health care covered in a lifetime.[75] The Congressional Budget Office and Joint Committee on Taxation predicted that the insurance coverage provisions of the ACA will cost nearly $1.1 trillion over the period from 2012 to 2021. However, this cost was expected to be offset by $0.4 trillion earned back through penalty payments, an excise tax on high-premium insurance plans, and other increases in tax revenues.[76] Nonetheless, a 2011 McKinsey report questioned the effectiveness of such penalty payments, with data showing that for some employers it would be more cost-effective to pay the $2,000-per-employee penalty rather than pay for employees' insurance policies.[77]

The penalty tax is the reinvented form of the individual mandate, which required Americans to purchase health insurance. Although such a mandate may have been unconstitutional, the Supreme Court reframed the mandate

73 Melissa Thomasson, "Health Insurance in the United States," Economic History Association, April 17, 2003, http://eh.net/encyclopedia/article/thomasson.insurance.health.us.
74 Mike Sacks, "Supreme Court Health Care Decision: Individual Mandate Survives," The Huffington Post, June 28, 2012, http://www.huffingtonpost.com/2012/06/28/supreme-court-health-care-decision_n_1585131.html.
75 "Affordable Care Act: The New Healthcare Law at Two Years," The White House, http://www.whitehouse.gov/sites/default/files/uploads/careact.pdf.
76 "Updated Estimates for the Insurance Coverage Provisions of the Affordable Care Act," Congressional Budget Office, March 2012, http://www.cbo.gov/publication/43076.
77 Shubham Singhal, Jeris Stueland, and Drew Ungerman, "How U.S. Health Care Reform Will Affect Employee Benefits," *McKinsey Quarterly*, McKinsey & Company, June 2011, http://www.mckinseyquarterly.com/How_US_health_care_reform_will_affect_employee_benefits_2813.

to be enacted as a tax that must be paid if an individual does not have health care insurance.[78] Although this aspect of PPACA was arguably one of the most divisive, John McDonough, director of Harvard's Center for Public Health Leadership, has argued that the Act is actually remarkably similar to the Massachusetts health care law. According to McDonough, one of the four pillars of the Massachusetts plan is a tax penalty on those who can afford to buy health care but choose not to do so, a concept that is markedly similar to the penalty tax proposed by PPACA.[79]

PPACA's second major tool to improve coverage access is Medicaid expansion. The Act expands the pool of individuals eligible for Medicaid, such as low-income adults with no children. It also targets state-to-state variability by mandating that all individuals who earn less than 133 percent of the federal poverty level be considered eligible for Medicaid. The proposed Medicaid expansion has been the subject of controversy because the federal government has threatened to withhold Medicaid funding from states that do not expand their Medicaid coverage nets.

Third, in an effort to provide health care safety nets for as many Americans as possible, PPACA also introduces high-risk insurance pools. These pools are organized by the state in order to meet the needs of high-risk individuals who do not have access to group health care insurance (such as through an employer or a family member's employer). High-risk insurance pools are not different from regular insurance provisions except in the way that they cater to a very specific population, and members can access their health care benefits in a manner similar to people enrolled in regular insurance schemes.[80]

These health care exchanges are the most expensive aspect of the bill. According to CBO, the state health care exchanges and related costs are expected to total more than $777 billion from 2012 to 2021.[81] Dr. Charles Blahous, senior research fellow at George Mason University's Mercatus Center, raised concerns that from the current vantage point it is very difficult to predict the participation rates of such programs. As the cost of an insurance pool would be determined primarily by participation rates, this aspect of the program is tenuous at best, according to Blahous.[82]

Finally, in a move that may completely change the health care industry, PPACA denounces the fee-for-service (FFS) model, which is the basis of many existing insurance plans. The main cause for concern is that the FFS model often renders health care unreachable due to the high cost of referrals and medical tests that may be unnecessary. In place of FFS, the Act prescribes bundled payments, through which payments are made to health care providers for the complete, quality care of a patient, from start to finish.

The path to the Affordable Care Act was not travelled without toil and trouble. Politicking within Congress had a huge influence on the shape and direction that health care reform took, and, even now, political factionalism threatens to undermine the goals that the Act aims to achieve. While Democrats support the Act for its net coverage, Republicans argue that the Act will hurt the economy more than it will improve health care outcomes.

78 Adam Liptak, "Supreme Court Upholds Health Care Law, 5-4, in Victory for Obama," *The New York Times*, June 28, 2012, http://www.nytimes.com/2012/06/29/us/supreme-court-lets-health-law-largely-stand.html.

79 Liz Halloran, "'Obamneycare' Revisited: Tax Penalties Most Similar Part, Expert Says," National Public Radio, July 5, 2012, http://www.npr.org/blogs/itsallpolitics/2012/07/05/156302382/obamneycare-revisited-tax-penalties-most-similar-part-expert-says.

80 "Consumer Guide To High-Risk Health Insurance Pools," National Association of Health Underwriters, http://www.nahu.org/consumer/HRPGuide.cfm.

81 "Updated Estimates for the Insurance Coverage Provisions of the Affordable Care Act," Congressional Budget Office, March 2012, http://www.cbo.gov/publication/43076.

82 Charles Blahous, "Fiscal Consequences of the Affordable Care Act," The Mercatus Center at George Mason University, 2012, http://mercatus.org/sites/default/files/publication/The-Fiscal-Consequences-of-the-Affordable-Care-Act_1.pdf.

Insurance companies have also not been in favor of the program, presumably due to the stringent conditions that PPACA will place on premiums and coverage. There are other parties involved as well, such as hired lobbyists and the American Medical Association.

Looking Ahead

The effects of the Affordable Care Act, in many ways, have yet to be seen. CBO analysis from March 2010 predicted that the Act would reduce the federal deficit by $108 billion by 2019.[83]

More recently, the CBO released revised budget forecasts based on the Supreme Court decision. Their analysis showed that the decision would make the Act $84 billion less expensive, which amounts to about 7 percent of the total projected cost of the Act.[84] On the other hand, state governors, who say that their state economies simply cannot handle the costs of Medicaid expansion, are turning down the suggested Medicaid expansion. The current numbers will change frequently as the multiple phases of the ACA come into action.

What is clear is that in its effort to control health care costs and, over time, the national deficit, PPACA will impact the budgets of many government agencies. Yet the Act operates on the belief that in order to stimulate change in one system, it is necessary to bring about change in the others. With the recent symbolic House repeal of the Affordable Care Act, it is clear that the debate is not over.[85] Only time will tell whether the ACA is actually the medicine for Americans who wish that good health were not a decision, but a right.

83 Douglas Elmendorf, letter to Senator Harry Reid, Congressional Budget Office, March 11, 2010, http://www.cbo.gov/sites/default/files/cbofiles/ftpdocs/113xx/doc11307/reid_letter_hr3590.pdf.

84 "Estimates for the Insurance Coverage Provisions of the Affordable Care Act Updated for the Recent Supreme Court Decision," Congressional Budget Office, July 24, 2012, http://www.cbo.gov/publication/43472.

85 Andrea Seabrook, "House Repeals Affordable Care Act In Symbolic Vote," National Public Radio, July 11, 2012, http://www.npr.org/2012/07/11/156629620/house-repeals-affordable-care-act-in-symbolic-vote.

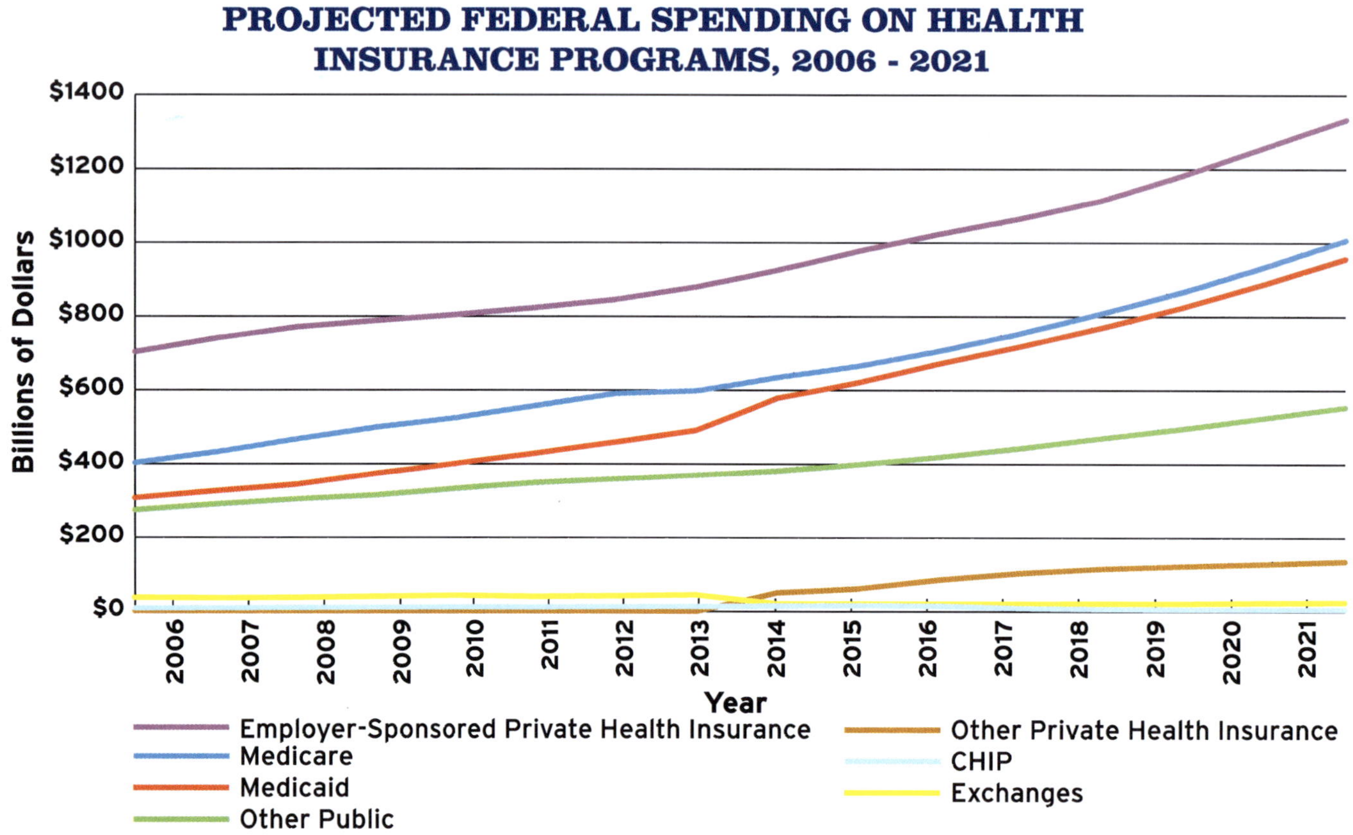

FIGURE 24

SOURCE: Centers for Medicare and Medicaid Services, http://www.cms.gov/Research-Statistics-Data-and-Systems/Statistics-Trends-and-Reports/NationalHealthExpendData/Downloads/Proj2011PDF.pdf.

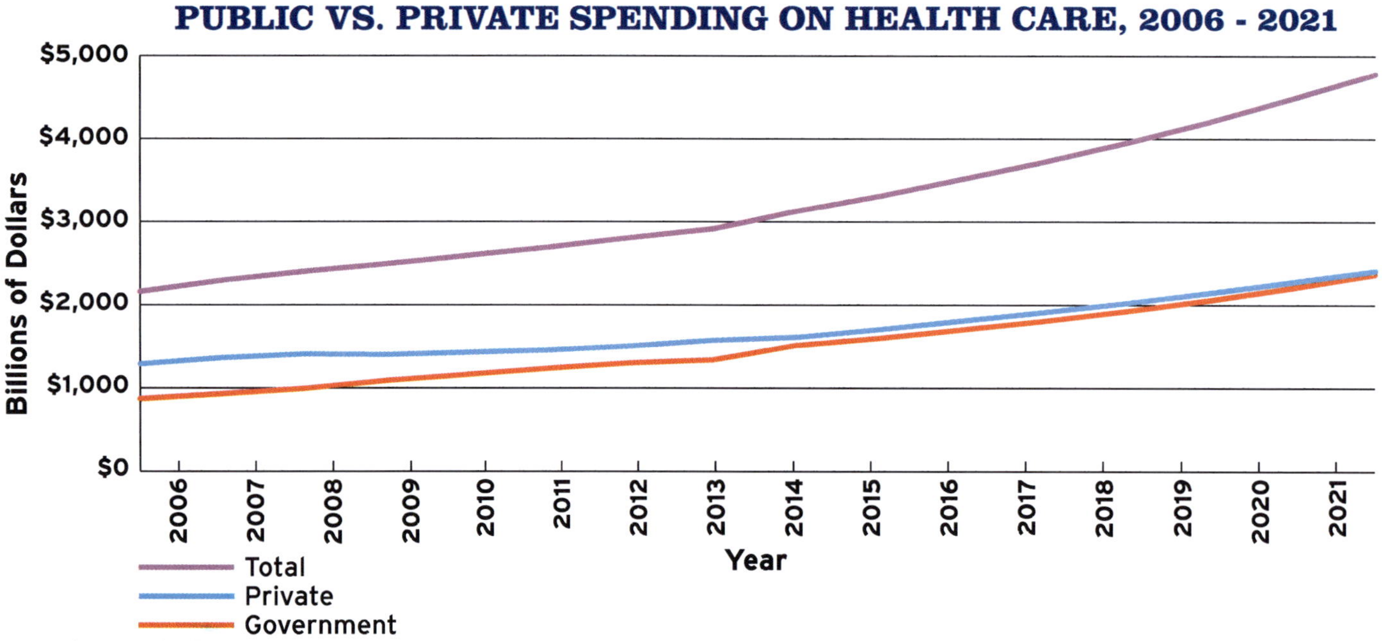

FIGURE 25

SOURCE: Centers for Medicare and Medicaid Services, http://www.cms.gov/Research-Statistics-Data-and-Systems/Statistics-Trends-and-Reports/NationalHealthExpendData/Downloads/Proj2011PDF.pdf.

★

ENTITLEMENT SPENDING: MEDICARE

by Christine Hurd and Alex Palmer

The alphabet soup of Medicare can be described as follows. Part A, Hospital Insurance, covers inpatient hospital stays. For example, if a person breaks a leg and needs to go through rehabilitation in a residential facility, Part A covers this treatment. Part B is called Medical Insurance and provides coverage for day-to-day needs that covers around 80 percent of general physicals and outpatient care, such as physical therapy. In 1965, these two Parts were all the government provided through Medicare: a single-payer health care system in which people paid a tax from wages earned over 10 years and were guaranteed insurance at age 65.

In 1997, over thirty years after original Medicare was implemented, Part C, known as Medicare Advantage, was passed and gave Medicare enrollees the option of receiving Medicare services through a private plan that the federal government would subsidize.

Finally, Part D, the Prescription Drug Plan, was enacted in 2003 and went into effect in 2006. It requires enrollees to pay a $295 deductible and covers 75 percent of further drug costs up to $2,700. If someone buys $2,700 worth of prescription drugs (paying $896.25) and requires more prescriptions, then they must pay 100 percent of the cost until they reach $6,154 worth of prescriptions. Then, what is lightly termed as "catastrophic coverage" ensues and the beneficiary only pays 5 percent of further costs.

MEDICARE SPENDING, 1966 - 2012 (real)

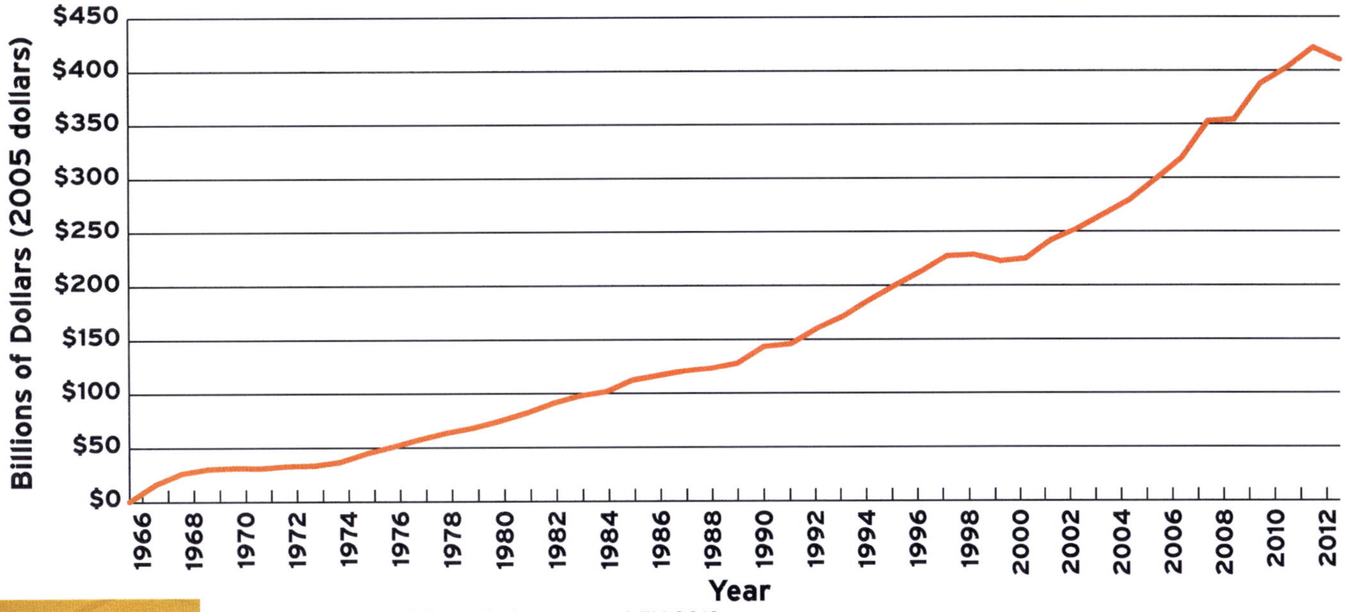

FIGURE 26 SOURCE: Budget of the U.S. Government FY 2013, http://www.gpo.gov/fdsys/pkg/BUDGET-2013-TAB/xls/BUDGET-2013-TAB-3-2.xls.

The changes to Medicare introduced by the Patient Protection and Affordable Care Act (PPACA), sometimes called "Obamacare," are complex and still in flux. At the core of these changes, though, is an emphasis on increasing prescription drug coverage while decreasing spending on Medicare Part C.

HEALTH AND POLITICS

Medicare has often been a political talking point for both Democrats and Republicans due to the massive size of the program and the high voting rates of the elderly, especially in swing states such as Florida.

Recent calls by Republicans to privatize Medicare or do away with it entirely are relatively new. President George W. Bush, for example, signed Medicare Part D into law. "Our government," Bush said at the time, "is finally bringing prescription drug coverage to the seniors of America."

Among the 2012 nominees for President and Vice President, there were three plans for reforming Medicare. President Obama's plan for Medicare, found most clearly in PPACA, centered on reducing Part C spending. In contrast, Governor Romney's plan proposed scaling back benefits for future seniors, leaving those seniors already enrolled in Medicare unaffected. Romney's proposed Medicare reforms would have also put forward a set of options in which Medicare remained a government program, but in conjunction with subsidized private firms that also offer health insurance—in essence, a reinstatement of Part C. Finally, Congressman Paul Ryan's plan was the most unconventional of the three, although he modified his stance upon accepting the invitation to be Romney's running mate. While Rep. Ryan originally supported a complete elimination of Medicare in its traditional form, Ryan's plan became more moderate during the campaign, allowing for a public option rather than solely a voucher system.

MEDICARE AND PPACA

In its long-term spending outlook, the Congressional Budget Office (CBO) predicts that Part D will become the fastest-growing part of the Medicare budget. Over 10 years, the CBO predicts, spending for Part D will almost triple, from $65.8 billion to $183 billion, while neither Part A nor Part B will even double. Part of this monumental increase is due to the elimination, under PPACA, of the uncovered area between $2,700 and $6,154 in prescription drug spending, because many seniors simply stopped following their treatment once they reached $2,700 in spending. Now, the government will cover 50 percent of prescription drug costs even beyond $2,700, encouraging those who require drugs to keep purchasing them, forcing more subsidization and, thus, higher costs.

While Part D spending will increase as a percent of overall Medicare spending, Part C (Medicare Advantage) will decrease. In April 2012, President Obama launched a demonstration project for postponement of the cuts to Medicare Advantage that PPACA enacted. Unsurprisingly, in the lead-up to the 2012 presidential election, some conservative leaders attributed this decision to the high concentration of Medicare Advantage recipients in swing states. Nevertheless, after the $8.35 billion project, the eventual cost of Group Plans (including Medicare Advantage) will increase from $131.9 billion to $152.4 billion over a decade, thereby increasing in absolute terms but decreasing as a percentage of total Medicare spending. This is because Medicare Advantage plans cost more than Medicare Parts A and B, though costs will not grow as quickly as costs for Part D.

Under Medicare Advantage, the government pays private insurers based on two factors: what county the beneficiary lives in (for cost of living considerations) and the Five-Star Quality Rating System score (though plans rarely receive below 2.5 stars). While original Medicare plans cost around $650 per month per beneficiary, Medicare

Advantage plans can cost up to $950 per month. Thus, PPACA, in original execution, was supposed to control these costs by leveling out the amounts paid.

WHAT GOES IN MUST COME OUT

Just as important as Medicare spending is Medicare revenue. For Americans younger than 65 years old, the only payment to Medicare is a 2.9 percent payroll tax, split equally between employees and their employers, and a 0.9 percent "Additional Medicare Tax" for high-income individuals that was created by PPACA.

Currently, the payroll tax pays for approximately of all of Medicare's expenses. Over time, though, the percentage of Medicare funded by this continuing 2.9 percent tax will fall to about one-third of the total cost under PPACA, according to the Medicare Trustee's report. Part of the reason for this fall in the percentage of total Medicare costs covered by the payroll tax is the increase in funding to Part D through other sources of revenue.

Part A is funded by the Hospital Insurance (HI) trust fund, while Parts B and D are funded by the Supplementary Medical Insurance (SMI) Trust Fund.

General Revenue Transfers

The Medicare Trustees report for 2012 predicted that Medicare expenses will reach nearly 7 percent of GDP by 2076. However, most of these increasing costs are covered by sources of revenue such as payroll taxes, state fees, and general revenue transfers. General revenue transfers are the funds the federal government gives to state Medicare programs through the federal budget. These will rise to support about 75 percent of Parts B and D over the next fifty years. In some ways, this isn't problematic, as both Parts B and D are reset every year and thus cannot be subject to a "run-away" budget item; Part A, on the other hand, presents a more difficult case.

The Problem with Part A

Though a Medicare Trustees report predicting an early death of the Hospital Insurance trust fund in 2024 caused a media scare, it is important to note that people have been predicting Medicare's death since its birth. Though the United States finds itself in a perilous fiscal position, the death of Medicare will not come suddenly or dramatically, but rather slowly, over a period of many years.

However, if Medicare spending continues to increase, new sources of revenue, possibly including new tax revenue, will need to be collected. Recent claims that such a tax increase would be a back-breaking burden on young Americans, though, go too far. While the deference given to seniors and other current voters to the detriment of future generations is a serious political problem, the challenges to Medicare are not insurmountable. If the payroll tax were raised to cover the future deficit and make the trust fund solvent in the long-term, then people born after 1990 would have to pay $4,000 extra in taxes over their lifetime while people who have already qualified for Medicare would receive all benefits in full with no additional tax paid.

The debate over Medicare spending and tax rates is also better understood when put into the context of taxes and spending in other developed nations. In the United States in 2007, the government funded 44.7 percent of all of

Medicare and Medicaid. Compared to other developed countries, in which governments can cover as much as 80 percent of national health spending, spending levels in the United States seem relatively low.

THE UNSURE SOLUTIONS

While a tax is one possible solution, there are also a number of demographics-based opportunities for the strains on Medicare to be eased. One of the more interesting indicators of this is the fertility rate projections for eventual Medicare solvency. If fertility rates rise, trust funds will stay solvent longer, as there will be more young people paying into the system to provide benefits for older generations. If life expectancy rises, then costs will rise, as Americans require more and more health care in old age. Thus, there are a number of factors that will strongly influence total Medicare costs in the coming years but are difficult to predict.

There are also technical considerations regarding long-term Medicare costs. If the American medical community can transition away from chronic tests, last-minute interventions, and expensive treatments in favor of preventive care and better general wellness practices, Medicare spending will likely decrease in the long-term. If current health trends—rising obesity rates, higher rates of diabetes and cardiovascular disease, and an emphasis on medication and surgery over more holistic approaches—continue, though, more and more health spending will be required, precipitating a demographic and fiscal crisis for the United States. Thus, more so than in any other area, the debate over Medicare spending combines two of the most pressing issues facing the country: the health of its citizens and the health of the federal budget. Controlling Medicare spending could be a first step toward solving both problems.

★

by Sandra Korn

FUNDING UNEMPLOYMENT COMPENSATION

The majority of federal money that goes to non-federal workers is provided through unemployment compensation: $103.8 billion in FY 2011.

Unemployment compensation is one of the only federal programs to be funded almost entirely by taxes collected from employers by the federal and state governments, which split the costs of funding state unemployment compensation programs.

If unemployment rates in a state are high enough, federal laws stipulate that the state begin paying Extended Benefits (EB) to unemployed workers beyond the time in which they would expect to collect unemployment insurance. EB programs are generally funded half by state governments and half by the federal government. However, state governments can borrow money from the federal government for EB if they are unable to fund their own unemployment programs.

In the past few years, the federal government has funded an increasingly large proportion of EB.[86] According to estimates from the U.S. Department of Labor, states are expected to continue borrowing from the federal government for the next few years, but at reduced rates.

UNEMPLOYMENT RATE, 2002 - 2012

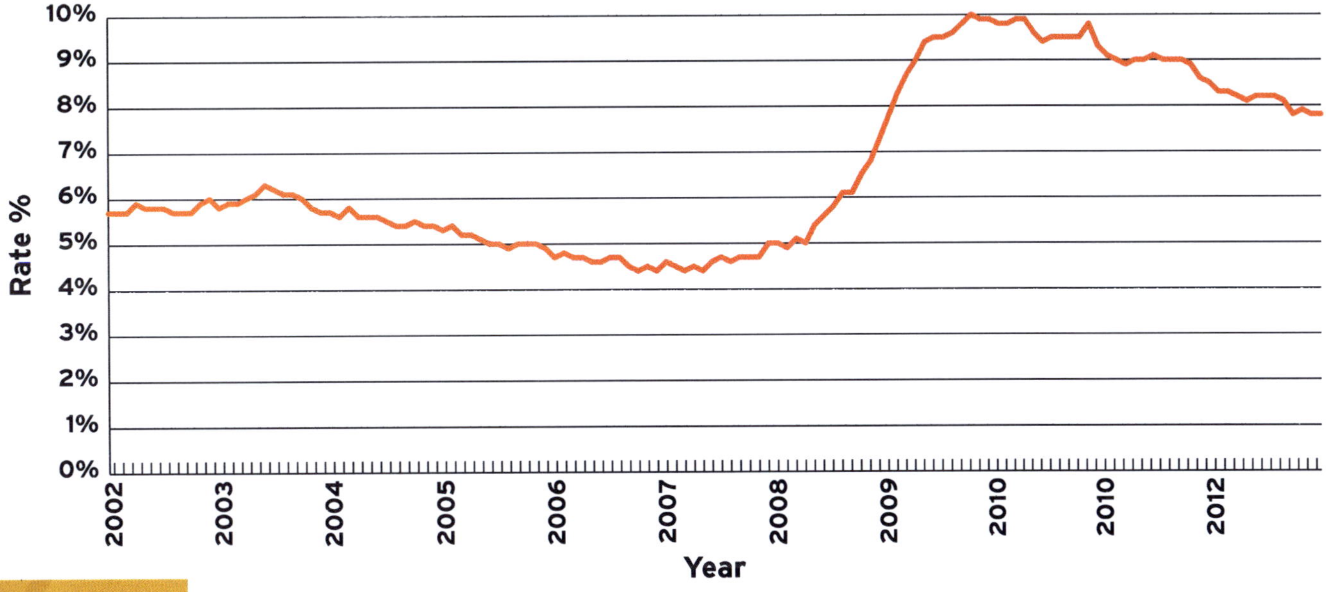

FIGURE 27 SOURCE: Bureau of Labor Statistics, http://data.bls.gov/timeseries/LNS14000000.

86 "UI Outlook," Employment and Training Administration, U.S. Department of Labor, February 13, 2012, http://workforcesecurity.doleta.gov/unemploy/pdf/prez_budget.pdf.

WHO GETS COMPENSATED?

The federal and state governments also work together to control how unemployment benefits are allocated in the United States. The federal government sets broad requirements for eligibility and duration, but most of the requirements for receiving unemployment compensation are dictated by states themselves.

The Bureau of Labor Statistics reported that 12.7 million Americans were unemployed in May 2012.[87] However, in the last week of May, only about 6 million Americans received unemployment benefits.[88] Thus the "insured unemployment rate," or the percentage of Americans receiving unemployment insurance, is substantially lower than the unemployment rate.

Of those unemployed Americans who did not qualify for insurance, many are temporary or self-employed workers; others are those who have just graduated from school. Others do not qualify for insurance because they were asked to leave their jobs because of misconduct or a labor dispute, or because they have criminal records. These workers may qualify for other social programs, like food stamps.

Not Eligible for UI?

Aaron Tanaka is the director of the Boston Workers' Alliance, a group that organizes around low-income workers' issues and provides counseling for unemployed workers in Boston. "Most people I see haven't been in a job for long enough to get unemployment," said Tanaka. "Also, [I see] people who were working and were let go. Often it's because of their CORI [Criminal Offender Record Information, Massachusetts's background check]."

Although these workers are unemployed, they do not qualify for unemployment insurance, either because of a past criminal record or because they have never found steady employment. They may depend on food stamps to survive, but if they don't qualify for those, either, these workers may find no support in the government's social safety net.

EXTENDING BENEFITS

Most significantly, however, jobless Americans can usually only receive benefits for about 26 weeks, depending on the state they live in. This term can be extended by the federal government for up to 99 weeks, especially in times of recession and persistent job loss. In 2011 and early 2012, as unemployment rates remained above 8 percent, American politicians searched for ways to bail out unemployed workers. In February 2012, the federal government extended unemployment insurance until the end of the year and temporarily extended payroll tax cuts for middle-class workers.[89]

However, the bill was controversial. Liberal politicians disliked the fact that it "paid" for this extra government spending by increasing the contribution that new government employees would have to put into their pension

87 "News Release: The Employment Situation—May 2012," Bureau of Labor Statistics, U.S. Department of Labor, June 1, 2012, http://www.bls.gov/news.release/archives/empsit_06012012.htm.

88 "Weekly Unemployment Claims Rise Modestly," *USA Today*, May 31, 2012, http://www.usatoday.com/money/economy/story/2012-05-31/1q-gdp-weekly-unemployment-benefits-claims/55301940/1.

89 Lucy Madison, "Congress Passes Extension of Payroll Tax Cut, Unemployment Benefits," CBS News, February 17, 2012, http://www.cbsnews.com/8301-503544_162-57380261-503544/congress-passes-extension-of-payroll-tax-cut-unemployment-benefits/.

plans. Democrats argued that this would hurt federal workers. Also, due to stipulations in the law, it has been hard for states to apply the federal government's extensions to the long-term unemployed.[90]

On the other hand, conservative politicians argued that more government spending was unnecessary and would keep unemployment rates higher for longer by removing incentives for unemployed people to get back to work. In fact, the debate over the February 2012 unemployment insurance bill echoed a common point of contention between conservative and liberal economists: how much spending is enough to relieve unnecessary suffering without being excessive?

FEDERAL SPENDING ON UNEMPLOYMENT COMPENSATION, 1976 - 2012 (real)

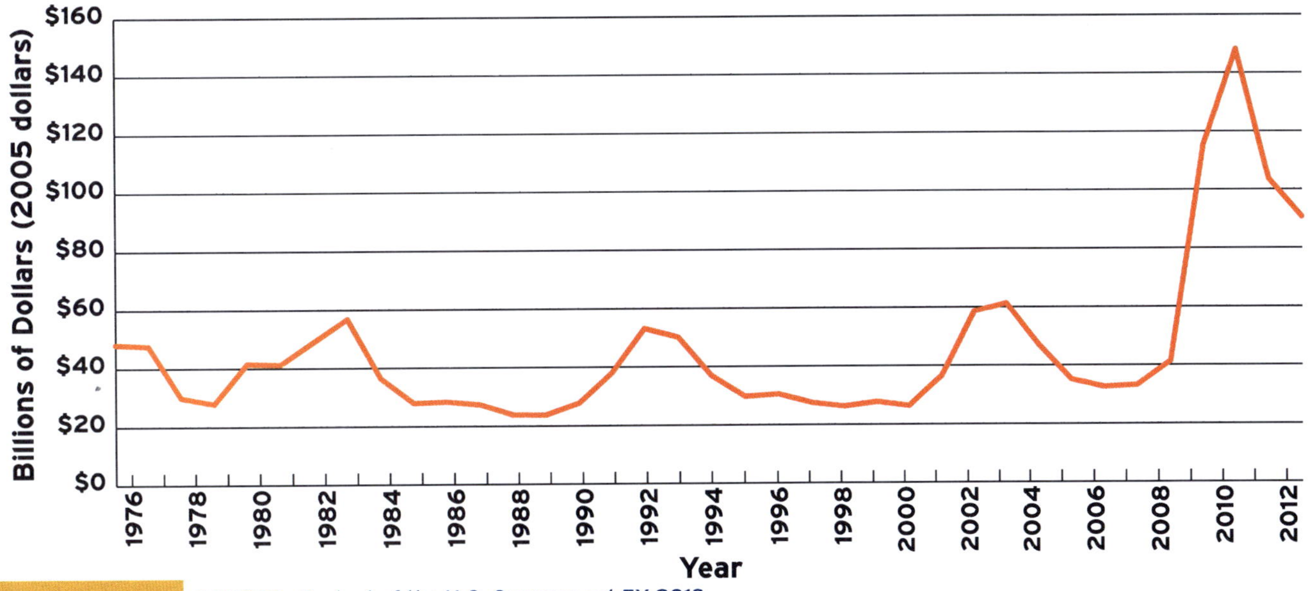

FIGURE 28 SOURCE: Budget of the U.S. Government FY 2013, http://www.gpo.gov/fdsys/pkg/BUDGET-2013-TAB/xls/BUDGET-2013-TAB-5-1.xls.

HOW MUCH IS "JUST ENOUGH"?

Conservatives have long argued that recessions call for business-friendly measures like tax cuts to encourage companies to create jobs and invest in the future. They note that increasing spending on unemployment insurance during a recession results in less job creation, because it increases the federal deficit (see below). Conservatives also reason that receiving unemployment insurance increases the duration of unemployment: by compensating unemployed workers, insurance can discourage workers from working hard to find new jobs and thus contribute to an elevated rate of unemployment. This is the reasoning behind work-search requirements, which stipulate that workers must be actively seeking work in order to qualify for unemployment insurance.

Does UI Slow Job Creation in a Recession?

YES **Michael Tanner**, director of health and welfare studies at the Cato Institute, a libertarian think-tank: "We are having one of the slowest recoveries, and one of the reasons is the debt overhanging this

90 Shaila Dewann, "U.S. Winds Down Longer Benefits for the Unemployed," *The New York Times*, May 28, 2012, http://www.nytimes.com/2012/05/29/business/economy/extended-federal-unemployment-benefits-begin-to-wind-down.html.

country. Businesses that are forward-looking see that the debt we have will turn into taxes down the road and refrain from investing in jobs."

NO **Jesse Rothstein,** professor at the University of California, Berkeley: "Right now the real constraint on [the unemployment rate] is not the workers searching for jobs. The jobs aren't there. As long as the jobs aren't there . . . it doesn't matter how hard people search, it's going to be equally hard to find jobs. As the labor market starts to recover and as employers start looking for workers, it's feasible to expect people to start looking for jobs."

Liberals note that during slow economic times, workers may simply be unable to find jobs. They reason that those who are not poor enough to qualify for programs like food stamps nonetheless require government support to pay their bills and continue purchasing consumer goods.[91]

These debates have led federal and state governments into a balancing act, as they strive to provide benefits for long enough to help workers struggling to make ends meet while not "rewarding" unemployment.

★

91 Jesse Rothstein, "Unemployment Insurance and Job Search in the Great Recession," *Brookings Papers on Economic Activity* 43, no. 2 (Fall 2011): 143-213, http://www.brookings.edu/~/media/Files/Programs/ES/BPEA/2011_fall_bpea_papers/2011_fall_bpea_conference_rothstein.pdf.

THE SOCIAL SAFETY NET: WELFARE AND FOOD AID IN THE RECESSION

According to the National Bureau of Economic Research, the Great Recession ended in June 2009.[92] This will come as news to the 12.5 million Americans who were unemployed and actively seeking work in 2012, the 15 percent of Americans receiving food aid from the federal government, or the millions of other people who continued to struggle to make ends meet even after the recession was nominally finished.

The neediest Americans—those facing unemployment, severe debt, and poverty—depend on the federal social safety net to get by. Over the past year, as American families struggled to regain their financial footing, the federal government again spent billions of dollars providing relief and social services to its citizens. However, despite the number of families that are glad to benefit from these payments, the programs have continued to serve as the epicenter of an ongoing debate about the role of government and the rights of American citizens.

There is no precise definition of what the social safety net comprises. The federal government funds hundreds of social programs for Americans. Government spending on public education, housing assistance, health care (including Medicare and Medicaid), Social Security, and unemployment compensation are among the best known. Much of this funding goes to programs run by states. For example, the federal government provides grant money to state governments for family support services through the Promoting Safe and Stable Families program.[93] Table 10 highlights federal spending on various social safety net programs in FY 2012.

TABLE 10 - DISCRETIONARY SPENDING ON SELECTED SOCIAL SAFETY NET PROGRAMS

Program	FY 2012 spending ($ billion)
Food stamps	$85.1
Temporary Assistance for Needy Families and related programs	$17.4
Veterans education, training, and rehabilitation	$12.1
Foster care and adoption assistance	$6.9
Old-Age and Survivors Insurance (OASI)	$2.7
Homeless assistance	$2.3
Promoting Safe and Stable Families	$0.6

Most notably, the government's welfare and food aid programs are exceptionally important not only for poor and working-class American families but also for politicians concerned about excessive spending. The rest of this article will investigate the state of these programs and the political debates surrounding these aspects of the social safety net.

92 "'Great Recession' Over, Research Group Says," MSNBC, September 20, 2010, http://www.msnbc.msn.com/id/39269753/ns/business-eye_on_the_economy/t/great-recession-over-research-group-says/.
93 "All-Purpose Table—FY 2010-2012," Administration for Children and Families, U.S. Department of Health and Human Services, http://www.acf.hhs.gov/sites/default/files/assets/fy2012apt.pdf.

The Earned Income Tax Credit

In 2012, the federal government spent $52.25 billion on the Earned Income Tax Credit. The EITC is not exactly part of the social safety net; however, low- and middle-income families, especially if they have children, may be eligible for EITC, a refundable tax credit that may result in a family paying lower taxes or receiving a net tax refund.

The "Neverland" Beneath the Social Safety Net

Unfortunately, the "social safety net" doesn't catch everyone. While welfare was originally designed to help single mothers get by, an increasing number of mothers and other workers have fallen in the cracks between unemployment compensation, welfare, and food stamps, according to Randy Albeda, an economist at the University of Massachusetts, Boston.

"A lot of middle-class people or younger people who thought they would end up in decent jobs end up in this Neverland of low-income work because you make enough not to get cash assistance," said Albeda. "And low-income moms [who have found work] have been pushed up into [this Neverland]. In some ways it's a unifying factor, in other ways it's a dead space: you don't make enough to support yourself, but you're not eligible for any social protection."

HISTORY OF WELFARE

The U.S. government began its first coordinated effort to support poor families in the 1930s. Although laws had previously provided social services to the disabled and to veterans, the Social Security Act of 1935 represented the first attempt to provide relief to Americans who were simply poor. This law remains on the books, although it has been greatly amended in the past 80 years.

The most recent major revision to the American welfare system took place in 1996, when President Bill Clinton signed into law a bill that would, as he described it, "end welfare as we have come to know it." The Personal Responsibility and Work Opportunity Reconciliation Act ended the welfare program that was part of the Social Security Act and replaced it with a new program, Temporary Assistance to Needy Families (TANF). This change in legislation also heralded a change in the ideology underlying welfare.

Fearing "welfare dependency" and abuse of the social safety net, Clinton instituted welfare reforms that focused on providing aid to those who deserved it. Families receiving welfare payments would be required to look for work and find employment within two years of receiving payments, and they would only be eligible for federal welfare for a lifetime total of five years. This new system focused on households, especially those in which the head of household was a single mother, as the major recipients of benefits. In an effort to encourage the poor to look for work and send their children to school, it also ensured that families could not simply receive undeserved hand-outs. Because of Clinton's reform, welfare is no longer a full-fledged "entitlement" program, a program in which anyone qualifies for government support if they meet certain eligibility requirements. Instead, TANF is often temporary, as its name suggests. For example, the Illinois Department of Human Services website notes that to qualify for TANF, one must "develop a plan for becoming self-sufficient and follow it."[94] Likewise, Arizona named its state TANF program "Employing and Moving People off Welfare and Encouraging Responsibility" (EMPOWER).[95]

FARING WELL IN RECESSION

Because of these regulations as to who can receive TANF funding, welfare spending on the state level has not increased greatly during the recession. In 2012, the federal government will spend $17.4 billion on TANF and related programs; since welfare reform in 1996, the government's annual spending on TANF has never exceeded $20 billion.

This restricted flow of funding has hurt poor families. During the recession, they have faced rising rents and unemployment with roughly the same level of support from the federal government as before the economic crisis.[96] In fact, for various reasons, many families that previously depended on welfare relief are no longer eligible for TANF.

Albeda noted that, in theory, employment promotion stipulations would help single mothers escape dependency on welfare by encouraging employment and protecting them with the unemployment safety net if necessary. However, there is no evidence that this has happened. "What we see is the erosion of that particular safety [TANF] without any assurance that it's being replaced by another," like unemployment insurance, said Albeda.

THE POLITICS OF FOOD STAMPS

In total, the federal government was projected to spend $107.4 billion on food and nutrition assistance in FY 2012. In contrast to TANF, participation in these programs has increased dramatically in the past few years. The largest food aid program, known as the Supplemental Nutrition Assistance Program (SNAP), serves about 45 million Americans by providing food stamps that total a few hundred dollars per month.[97] In total, the program was projected to cost $88.2 billion in FY 2012.

Other food aid programs include the Special Supplemental Nutrition Program for Women, Infants, and Children (WIC), which provides assistance to pregnant women and mothers with small children. These other programs cost an additional $7 billion per year. Also, the federal government pays for such programs as the School Breakfast Program, the School Lunch Program, and the Nutrition Program for the Elderly.

SNAP is an entitlement program, which means that everyone who applies and meets eligibility requirements receives benefits. During the recession, when many families faced increased interest payments on debt and loss of income due to unemployment, SNAP provided necessary food assistance for America's poorest. A report by the

94 "Temporary Assistance for Needy Families (TANF)," Illinois Department of Human Services, http://www.dhs.state.il.us/page.aspx?item=30358.
95 Liz Schott, "Policy Basics: What is TANF?" Center on Budget and Policy Priorities, July 6, 2011, http://www.cbpp.org/cms/?fa=view&id=936.
96 Jason DeParle, "Welfare Limits Left Poor Adrift as Recession Hit," *The New York Times*, April 7, 2012, http://www.nytimes.com/2012/04/08/us/welfare-limits-left-poor-adrift-as-recession-hit.html.
97 "SNAP Monthly Data," Food and Nutrition Service, U.S. Department of Agriculture, http://www.fns.usda.gov/pd/34SNAPmonthly.htm; "Supplemental Nutrition Assistance Program: Number of Persons Participating," Food and Nutrition Service, U.S. Department of Agriculture, http://www.fns.usda.gov/pd/29snapcurrpp.htm.

Center on Budget and Policy Priorities noted that while TANF caseloads remained relatively stable or even fell in some states, SNAP caseloads rose 45 percent during the height of the recession.[98]

However, SNAP faces a difficult future. The Farm Bill, the legislation that governs subsidies and regulations for farms in the U.S., also includes provisions to fund food stamps for low-income Americans. Legislators have already decided that the next Farm Bill will include billions, if not tens of billions, in cuts to SNAP.

Food Stamps in Food Deserts

Recent discussions about food aid have focused on the ability of families on food stamps to access nutritious and sustainable food. The persistence of food deserts, or areas with few healthy food options, in low-income neighborhoods means that many people on food stamps are unable to buy healthy meals. Increasingly, states and towns are investigating programs that will allow families to use food stamps at farmers' markets.[99] These programs make it possible for farmers to accept SNAP benefits by implementing Electronic Benefit Transfer (EBT), the system by which SNAP benefits are issued, at farmers' markets.

In May 2012, the U.S. Department of Agriculture's Food and Nutrition Service allocated $4 million for states to set up equipment in farmers' markets so that farmers could accept food stamps for payment.[100] A similar program is being discussed for inclusion in the upcoming Farm Bill. These plans will hopefully boost business for local farmers while also increasing the ability of Americans on food stamps to access sustainable and healthful food.

CONCLUSION

The role of the social safety net in America is constantly under debate. Republicans have criticized the so-called "cradle to grave service" of America's "welfare empire."[101] Democrats staunchly defend these social services because the safety net serves to protect millions of low-income Americans from hunger and deeper poverty.

Despite partisan debate, one thing that both parties can agree on is that the current social safety net is far from perfect. Critics on both the Right and the Left have called for the government's social programs to be more streamlined, for example, allowing families to access benefits through a single gateway as opposed to applying to a myriad of programs separately. Thus, both in agreement and disagreement, both major political parties will continue to make the social safety net a topic of debate and discussion.

98 LaDonna Pavetti and Liz Schott, "TANF's Inadequate Response to Recession Highlights Weakness of Block-Grant Structure," Center on Budget and Policy Priorities, July 14, 2011, http://www.cbpp.org/cms/?fa=view&id=3534.

99 "Food Stamps and EBT at Farmers Markets," Washington State Farmers Market Association, http://www.wafarmersmarkets.com/resources/foodstamps-market.html.

100 "Fiscal Year (FY) 2012 Funding To Increase Farmers' Market Participation in the Supplemental Nutrition Assistance Program," U.S. Department of Agriculture, May 2, 2012, http://www.fns.usda.gov/snap/rules/Memo/2012/FM_051112.pdf.

101 Peter Ferrara, "America's Ever Expanding Welfare Empire," *Forbes*, April 22, 2011, http://www.forbes.com/sites/peterferrara/2011/04/22/americas-ever-expanding-welfare-empire/.

COMPOSITION OF FEDERAL "INCOME-SECURITY" SPENDING, 1962 - 2012

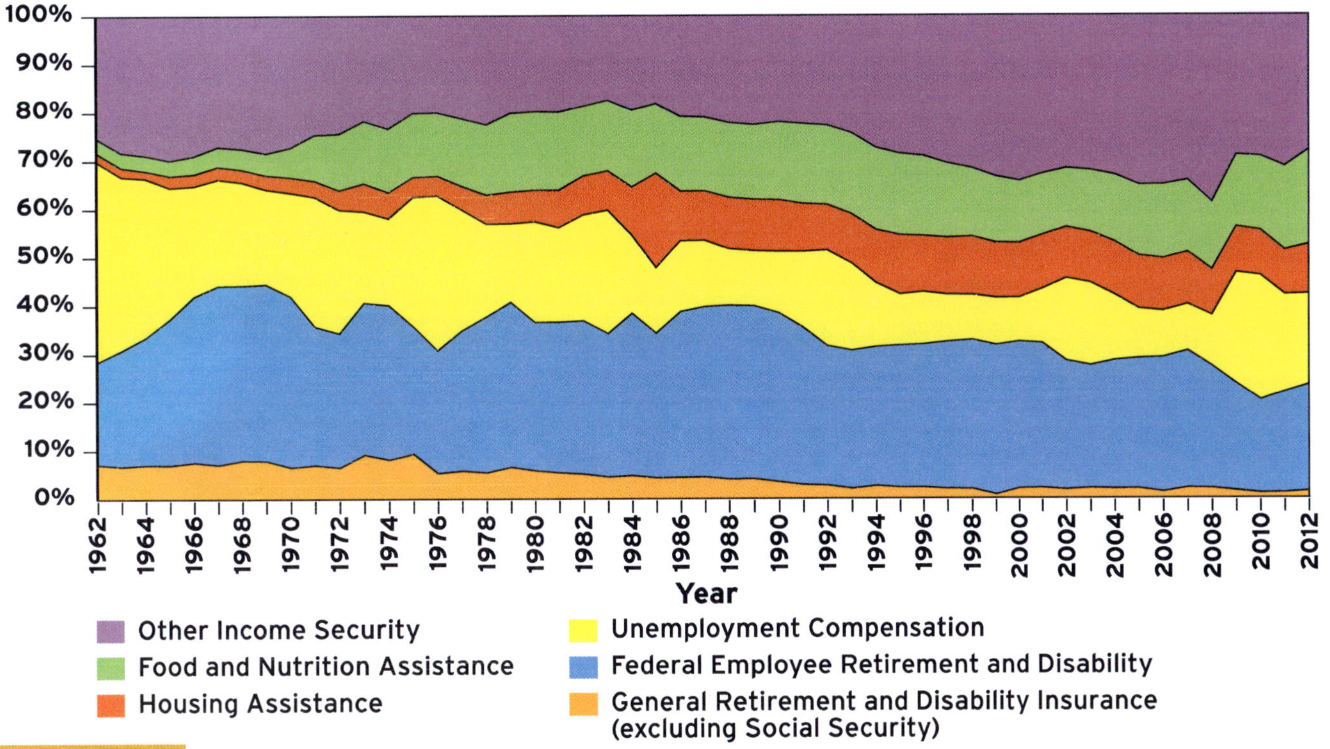

FIGURE 29

SOURCE: Budget of the U.S. Government FY 2013, http://www.gpo.gov/fdsys/pkg/BUDGET-2013-TAB/xls/BUDGET-2013-TAB-3-2.xls.

INCOME SECURITY SPENDING, 1962 - 2012 (real)

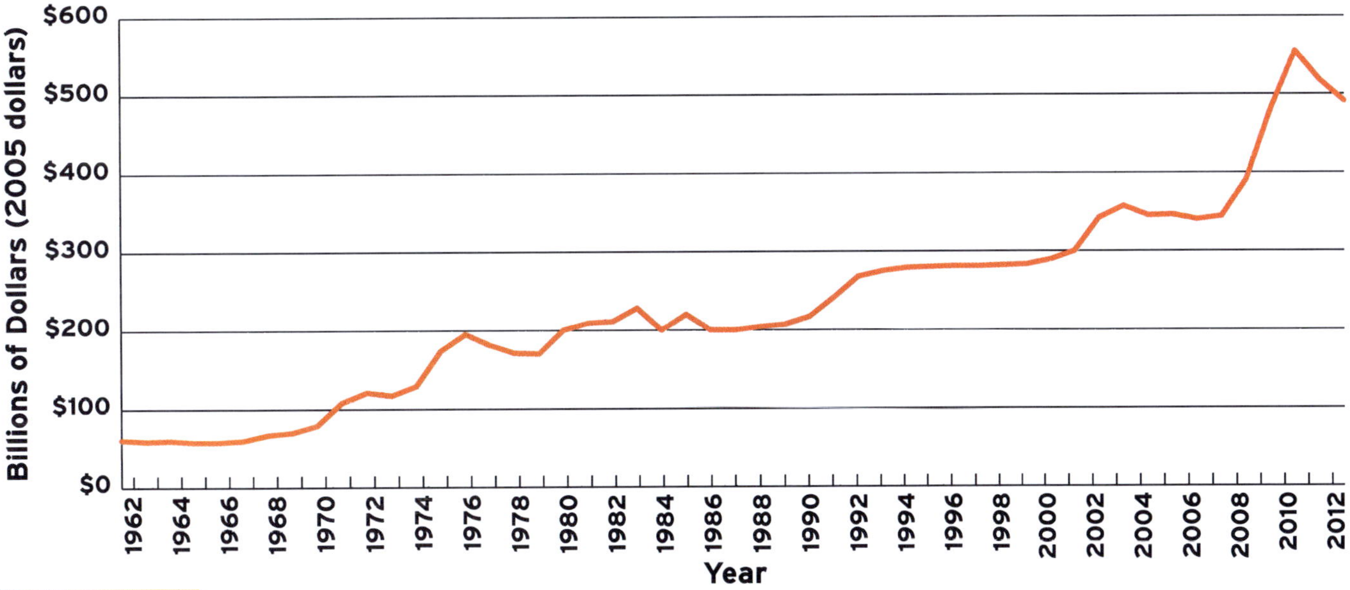

FIGURE 30

SOURCE: Budget of the U.S. Government FY 2013, http://www.gpo.gov/fdsys/pkg/BUDGET-2013-TAB/xls/BUDGET-2013-TAB-3-2.xls.

★

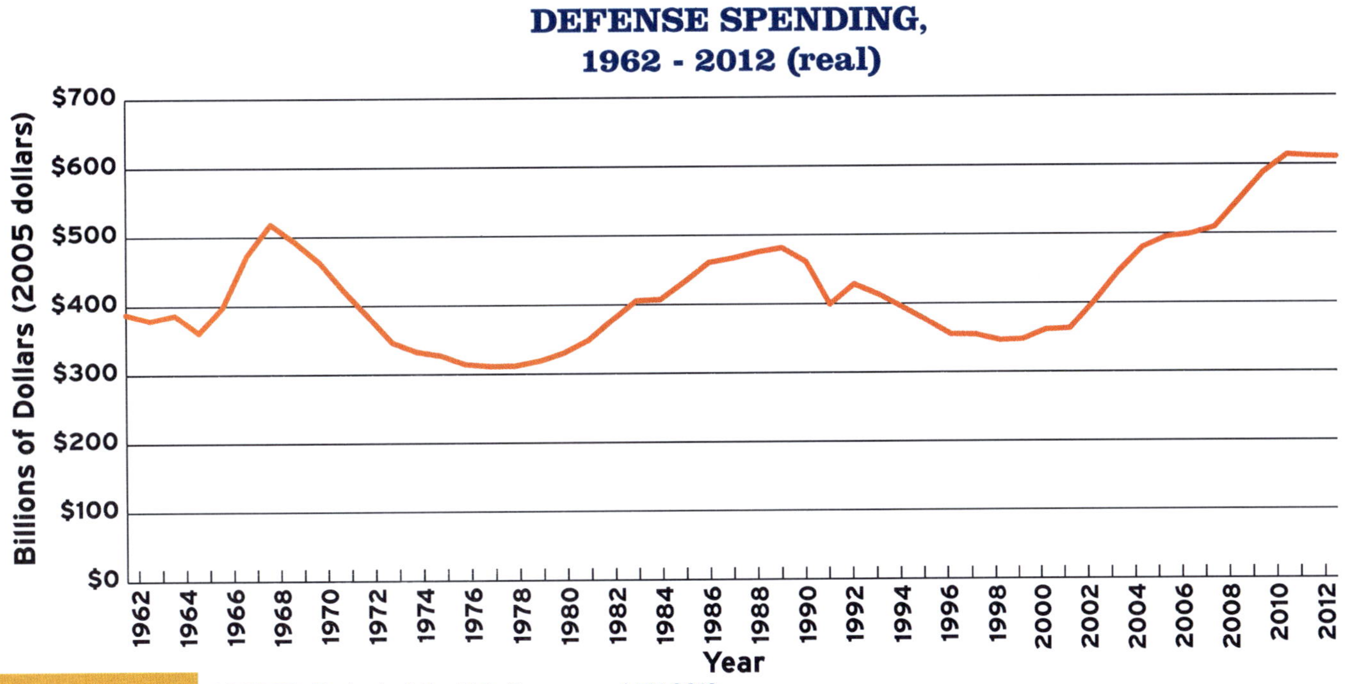

FIGURE 31

SOURCE: Budget of the U.S. Government FY 2013,
http://www.gpo.gov/fdsys/pkg/BUDGET-2013-TAB/xls/BUDGET-2013-TAB-3-2.xls.

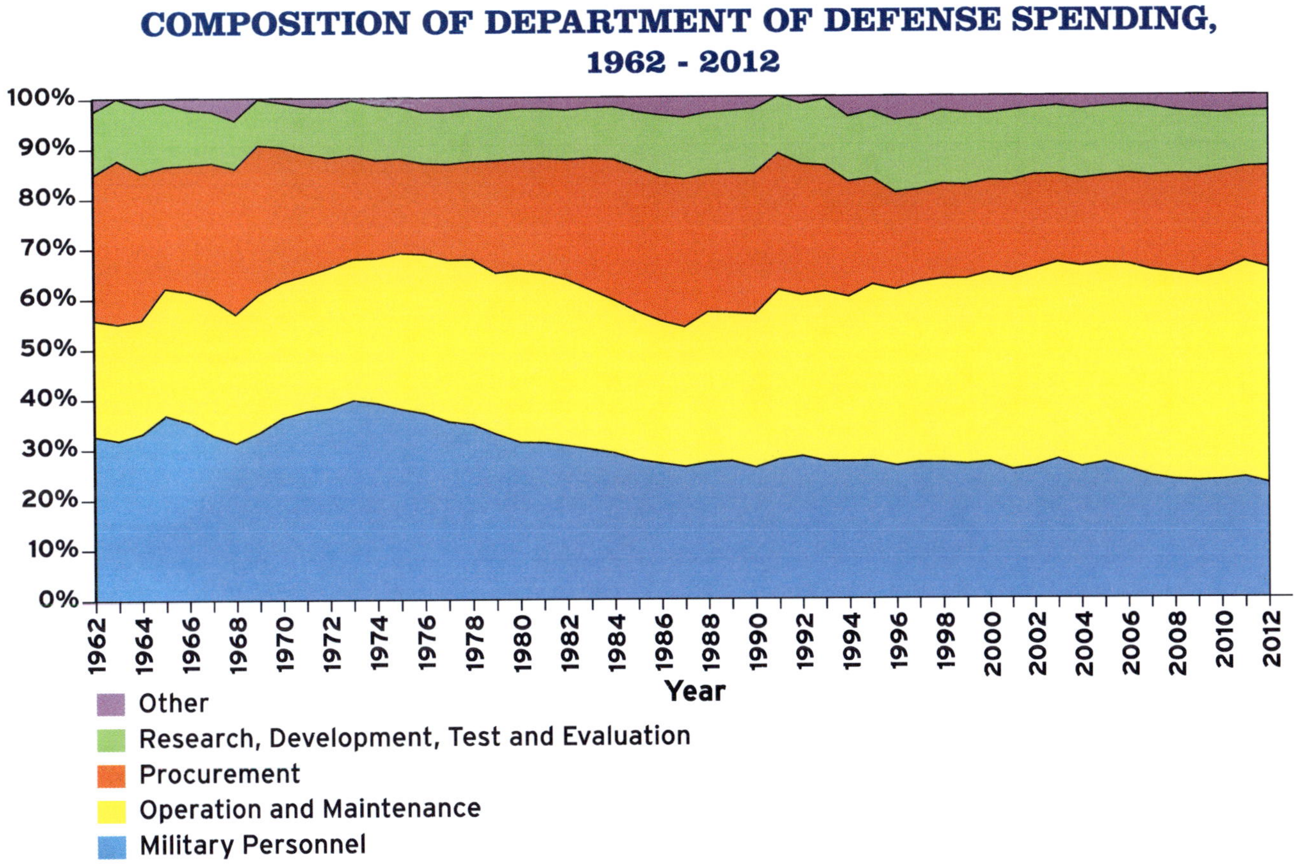

FIGURE 32

SOURCE: Budget of the U.S. Government FY 2013,
http://www.gpo.gov/fdsys/pkg/BUDGET-2013-TAB/xls/BUDGET-2013-TAB-3-2.xls.

COMPOSITION OF U.S. DEFENSE PERSONNEL, 2011 - 2013

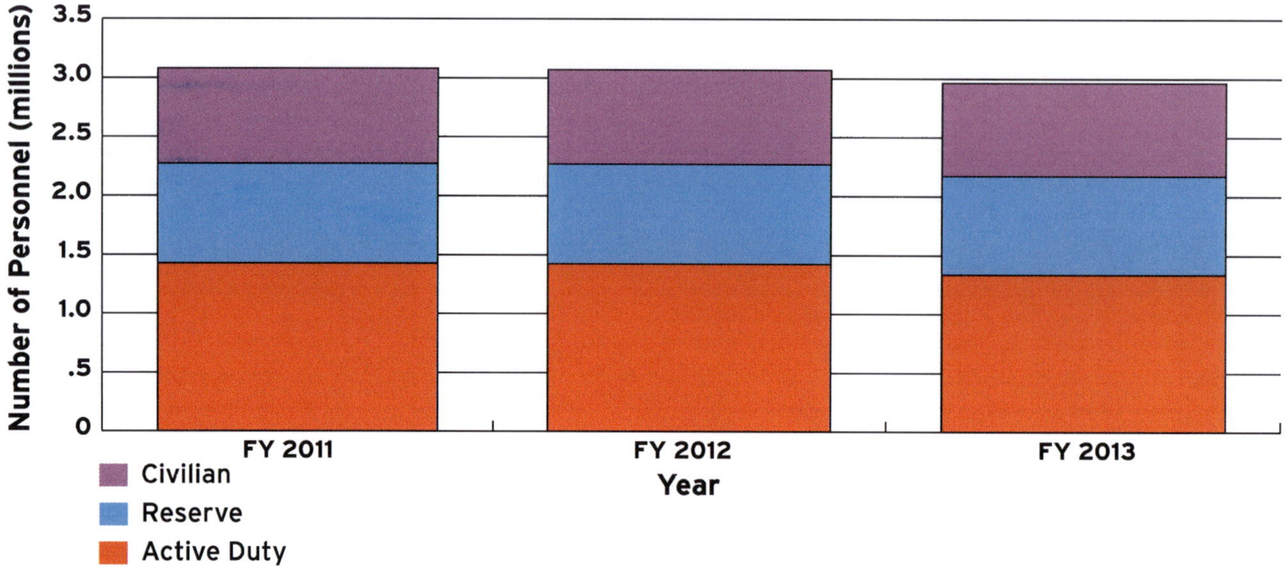

FIGURE 33 SOURCE: Department of Defense, http://comptroller.defense.gov/defbudget/fy2013/FY13_Green_Book.pdf.

CONTRACT OBLIGATIONS BY CATEGORY, 1990 - 2011

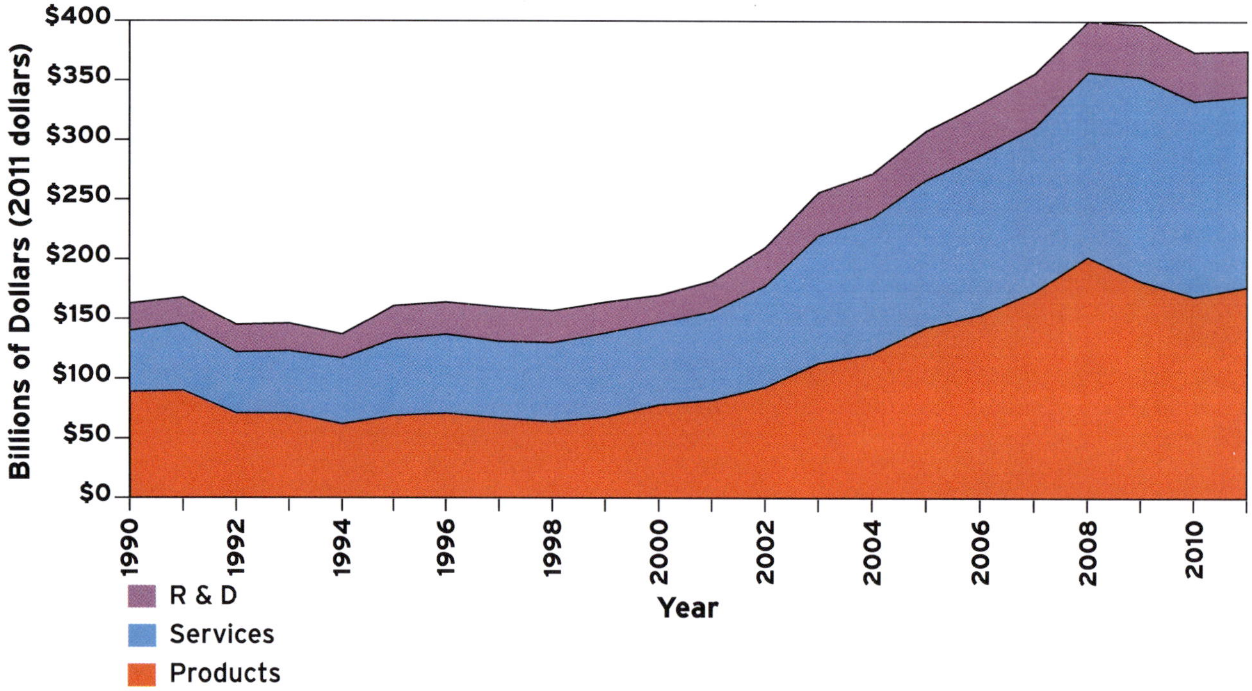

FIGURE 34 SOURCE: Center for Strategic and International Studies, http://csis.org/publication/us-department-defense-contract-spending-and-supporting-industrial-base.

★

FOREIGN RELATIONS & DEFENSE: Afghanistan and Iraq

by Andres Uribe

The terrorist attacks of September 11, 2001, ushered in a new era in the history of American military engagements. While the Clinton administration had deployed troops on peacekeeping and humanitarian missions in the Balkans, Haiti, and Somalia, the United States had not engaged in a full-scale military operation since the 1990-1991 Gulf War. By March 2003, America was embroiled in two wars that would eventually cost the nation thousands of lives and over $1.5 trillion and would dominate domestic politics and international relations for years to come.

Key Terms

Operation Enduring Freedom: Term used by the U.S. military to refer to operations under the umbrella of the "Global War on Terror." Enduring Freedom primarily refers to the war in Afghanistan that began in 2001 but also encompasses smaller-scale counterterrorism activities in other parts of the world.

Operation Iraqi Freedom/New Dawn: Operation Iraqi Freedom is the term used by the U.S. military to refer to the military engagement in Iraq that began in 2003. After August 2010, the operation's name was changed to New Dawn, to reflect the decreased role of U.S. troops in the country.

Overseas Contingency Operations (OCO): Term that came to prominence during the Obama administration to replace "Global War on Terror"; has been broadened to include Operation Iraqi Freedom/ New Dawn.

AFGHANISTAN - OPERATION ENDURING FREEDOM

The events of September 11, 2001, necessitated an immediate strategic and political response from the Bush administration. Unlike traditional threats to American security, the attacks that claimed nearly 3,000 lives that morning were not the work of a foreign government; the operation was rather conducted by al-Qaeda, a multi-national, stateless terrorist organization. Whereas retaliating against a foreign government is relatively straightforward because it is possible to locate governmental power, the Bush administration found itself pursuing an enemy with no official capital or headquarters.

Intelligence-gathering operations traced al-Qaeda's leadership to Afghanistan, where evidence indicated that the militant, extremist Taliban government was harboring and protecting the terrorist group. Less than a month after the 9/11 attacks, Operation Enduring Freedom opened with an aerial bombing campaign followed by the deployment of ground forces. U.S. ground troops began the operation in a support capacity, working with Afghan anti-Taliban forces. The capital, Kabul, and the southern Taliban stronghold of Kandahar both fell in late 2001.

As months passed, the mission expanded. The United Nations authorized an International Security Assistance Force (ISAF) of troops from 46 countries to form a coalition under U.S. command, and Enduring Freedom extended operations outside of Kabul and Kandahar.

Though American and allied forces controlled most of Afghanistan by early 2002, the Taliban continued aggressively recruiting fighters from its territory near the Afghanistan-Pakistan border to conduct an insurgency. Insurgent violence remained at a fairly constant level through 2006, a fact that was reflected in U.S. military spending: after requesting $20 billion for the war in Afghanistan in FY 2001 and 2002, the Department of

Defense (DoD) requested $14 billion in 2003, $12.3 billion in 2004, $17.2 billion in 2005, and $17.9 billion in 2006. The relatively minor variance in these numbers was matched, as is typically the case, by insignificant variation in troop levels through 2006. Troop levels increased steadily but slowly from 2001 to 2006, reaching 10,000 by 2002 and hovering around 20,000 in 2005 and 2006 (see Figure 35).

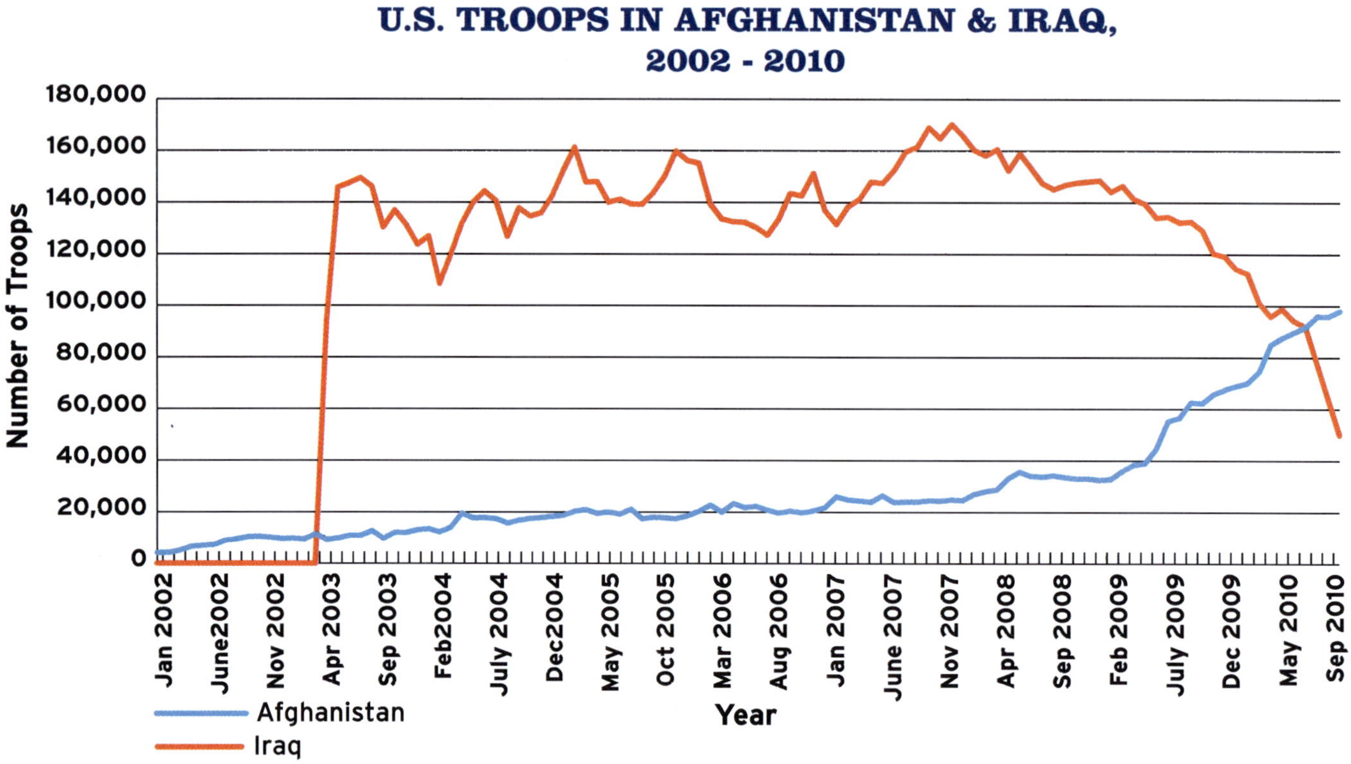

FIGURE 35 SOURCE: Congressional Research Service, http://www.fas.org/sgp/crs/natsec/RL33110.pdf.

In 2007, however, President Bush ordered a renewed offensive against the Taliban, supported by a moderate troop increase. In early 2008, this troop increase was expanded into a major surge, which continued into 2011. Troop levels reached 34,000 in 2008, 69,000 in 2009, and 98,000 in 2010. DoD spending in Afghanistan correspondingly increased, jumping to $37.2 billion in 2007, $40.6 billion in 2008, $56.1 billion in 2009, and $87.7 billion in 2010.[102] In 2011, following a successful operation to kill Osama bin Laden, the leader of al-Qaeda and the mastermind of the 9/11 attacks, President Obama announced a slow drawdown of troops from Afghanistan across 2011 and 2012.

This shrinking of the ground force has been accompanied, however, by a marked increase in Unmanned Aircraft Systems (UAS, commonly referred to as "drones") strikes in both Afghanistan and Pakistan, beginning in 2009. Drone attacks are politically controversial, and most information regarding the program is classified. DoD has released some basic data, however. Funding for research, development, and procurement of UAS doubled

102 Amy Belasco, "The Cost of Iraq, Afghanistan, and Other Global War on Terror Operations Since 9/11," Congressional Research Service, March 29, 2011, http://www.fas.org/sgp/crs/natsec/RL33110.pdf. It is worth noting that stable insurgent violence was not the only factor behind this lack of expansion in funding or troop presence from 2003 to 2006. The war in Iraq, which had begun in 2003, immediately gained political and strategic primacy over Afghanistan, a fact reflected in the allocation of military resources.

from 2010 to 2011, from $3 billion to nearly $6 billion. Overall flight hours by drones increased as well, from approximately 460,000 hours in 2009 to approximately 560,000 in 2010 and to an estimated 610,000 in 2011.[103]

The New America Foundation reported that the total number of drone strikes in Pakistan increased from 33 in 2008 to 53 in 2009 and 118 in 2010 before falling to 70 in 2011.[104] From this we can infer an increase in costs associated with the UAS program from 2008 to 2011, though knowing how much of an increase would require more data than is publicly available.

IRAQ - OPERATION IRAQI FREEDOM/NEW DAWN

The war in Iraq also followed, albeit less directly, from the September 11 terrorist attacks. The Bush administration claimed a connection between al-Qaeda and the Iraqi government of Saddam Hussein and argued that Hussein was pursuing the development of weapons of mass destruction; both claims were largely unsubstantiated, however, and were comprehensively disproved in the months and years following the invasion.

In March 2003, without the approval of the United Nations or the international community at large, the United States invaded Iraq, reaching the capital of Baghdad and felling the Hussein regime within five weeks. The conclusion of this invasion (marked by President George W. Bush's "Mission Accomplished" speech in May 2003) represented only the first stage in the war, however.

An insurgency sprang up immediately, initially composed primarily of members of Hussein's deposed Ba'ath party but swelling as the occupation triggered mass resentment. This insurgency steadily expanded through 2006; the invasion force, which had been drawn down to 124,000 in February 2004 after its peak of 149,000 in August 2003, fluctuated but overall grew through the beginning of 2007, when troop levels reached 132,000 (see Figure 35 above). DoD spending in Iraq grew steadily from $50 billion in 2003 to $56.4 billion in 2004, $83.4 billion in 2005, and $98.1 billion in 2006.[105]

In January 2007, President Bush announced an initiative to control burgeoning insurgent and sectarian violence that included a major troop surge. Troop levels increased to 170,000 in November 2007 before declining to 147,000 by July 2008. These troop level increases were predictably matched by funding increases. Iraqi Freedom funding jumped by $29.1 billion in 2007 to $127.2 billion and further increased to $138.5 billion in 2008.[106] By most accounts the surge worked, with DoD claiming a major decrease in overall violence and casualty rates by the beginning of 2009.[107]

In 2009, the new Obama administration began shifting focus to the training and arming of Iraqi security forces and the gradual drawdown of U.S. combat forces. Iraqi Freedom funding accordingly dropped to $92 billion in 2009 and $66.5 billion in 2010.[108] Members of the "coalition of the willing," nations that had voluntarily

103 Dyke Weatherington, "Future of Unmanned Aircraft Systems in a Fiscally Constrained Environment," U.S. Department of Defense, 2011, http://events.aviationweek.com/html/dtar11/0217_keynote_Weatherington.pdf.
104 "The Year of the Drone," New America Foundation, July 24, 2012, http://counterterrorism.newamerica.net/drones.
105 Belasco 2011.
106 Belasco 2011.
107 This decrease in violence is not necessarily solely attributable to the surge, however. Doug Ollivant, a senior fellow at the New America Foundation and Army planning officer in Baghdad at the time of the surge, said otherwise. Ollivant stated that conditions improved largely due to the decision of Sunni leaders to abandon al-Qaeda and ally with the United States, a decision made before the surge was implemented. See "As the Iraq War Ends, Reassessing The U.S. Surge," National Public Radio, December 16, 2011, http://www.npr.org/2011/12/16/143832121/as-the-iraq-war-ends-reassessing-the-u-s-surge.
108 Belasco 2011.

supported the American invasion in 2003, withdrew their troops in 2009. By September 2010, all combat brigades had been withdrawn from Iraq, with only 50,000 U.S. troops remaining to support Iraqi security forces, a 70 percent decrease from the peak level. The last combat troops withdrew from Iraq in December 2011.

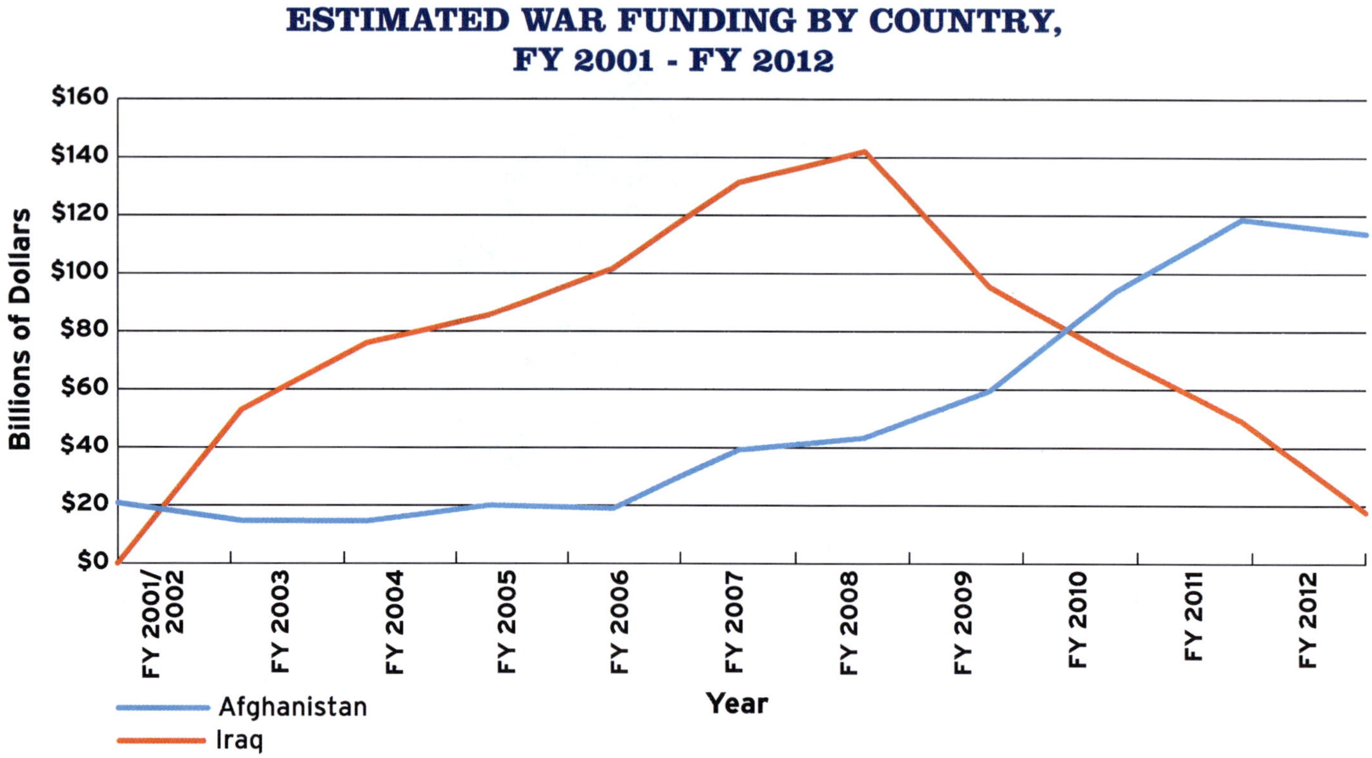

FIGURE 36 SOURCE: Congressional Research Service, http://www.fas.org/sgp/crs/natsec/RL33110.pdf.

SPENDING IN FY 2012

For FY 2012, President Obama requested $107 billion in budget authority for Operation Enduring Freedom and $11 billion for Post-Operation New Dawn (the successor to Operation Iraqi Freedom). The Office of Management and Budget summarized funding requested by the President for Enduring Freedom as being for "operations; force protection; reconstitution of damaged equipment; activities to counter and defeat improvised explosive devices; intelligence activities; and the training, equipping, and sustaining of the Afghan National Security Forces." It broke down New Dawn's requested budget authority as being aimed at "redeploying U.S. forces; transferring of responsibilities to Iraqis and U.S. civilian agencies; training, equipping, and advising Iraqi military and security forces; and supporting counterterrorism activities."[109]

The Department of Defense itself breaks down its budget requests by category of expenditure across both operations combined, as seen in Table 11. By far the largest category of OCO expenditure was Operations and Management, composing 52.0 percent of the overall outlay. This includes pay, mobilization, support, and deployment of troops. A small percentage of this allocation was assigned to Iraq to fund the Office of Security

109 "Overseas Contingency Operations," Budget of the U.S. Government FY 2012, http://whitehouse.gov/sites/default/files/omb/budget/fy2012/assets/overseas.pdf.

Cooperation, which continues to provide limited support to the Iraqi state; the majority went to ongoing combat operations in Afghanistan.[110]

The second-largest category is "Equipment Reset," which includes the replenishment and repair of equipment and munitions after combat operations, which amounted to 11.2 percent of costs. As a cost that is levied both during and after combat operations, it is relevant to both Enduring Freedom and New Dawn.

The third-largest allocation is funding for the "manning, training, equipping, operations, and sustainment" of the Afghanistan National Security Forces (ANSF), at $11.2 billion and 9.7 percent of total FY 2012 spending. Combined with the steady drawdown of troops in Afghanistan since 2011, the large amount of funding devoted to this category signals the Obama administration's attempt to shift the security burden away from the American military.

TABLE 11 - OCO BREAKDOWN, 2012 & 2013

	2012 (enacted)		2013 (requested)	
	$ billion	% of total	$ billion	% of total
Operations	$60.2	52.0%	$48.2	54.5%
Equipment Reset	$13.0	11.2%	$9.3	10.5%
Temporary End Strength	$2.2	1.9%	$6.1	6.9%
Afghanistan Security Forces Fund	$11.2	9.7%	$5.7	6.4%
Force Protection	$6.5	5.6%	$5.1	5.8%
Non-DoD Classified	$5.4	4.7%	$4.9	5.5%
Military Intelligence Program	$5.8	5.0%	$4.5	5.1%
Support for Coalition Forces	$2.1	1.8%	$2.2	2.5%
Improvised Explosive Devices Defeat	$2.4	2.1%	$1.7	1.9%
Afghanistan Infrastructure Fund	$0.4	0.3%	$0.4	0.5%
Commander's Emergency Response Program	$0.4	0.3%	$0.4	0.5%
Military Construction	$0.3	0.3%	--	--
Non-War/Other*	$5.8	5.0%	--	--
Total	**$115.7**	**100.0%**	**$88.5**	**100.0%**

SOURCE: "Overview: United States Department of Defense Fiscal Year 2013 Budget Request," U.S. Department of Defense, February 2012, http://comptroller.defense.gov/defbudget/fy2013/FY2013_Budget_Request_Overview_Book.pdf.

It is important to note that DoD funding does not represent total government expenditures in Afghanistan or Iraq. The Department of State and the United States Agency for International Development (USAID) carry out vital functions in both theaters, assisting in the consolidation of functioning, sovereign states and supporting economic development. Overseas Contingency Operations funding for these agencies remained fairly constant in Afghanistan from 2010 to 2012, increasing from $2.2 billion to $2.4 billion in 2011 but returning to $2.2 billion in 2012.

110 A similar, smaller category is "Force Protection," which consists of body and vehicle armor and mine resistance.

This consistency does not hold for Pakistan, however. In line with the focus on Pakistan that began to characterize U.S. policy beginning in 2011, State/USAID funding increased from $79 million in 2010 to $1.3 billion in 2011 before shrinking nominally in 2012. State/USAID funding for Iraq fell from $2.8 billion in 2010 to $1.7 billion in 2011 but jumped to $5.2 billion in 2012. In the context of a transition from a military- to a civilian-led political and economic mission, this major post-withdrawal increase makes sense.[111]

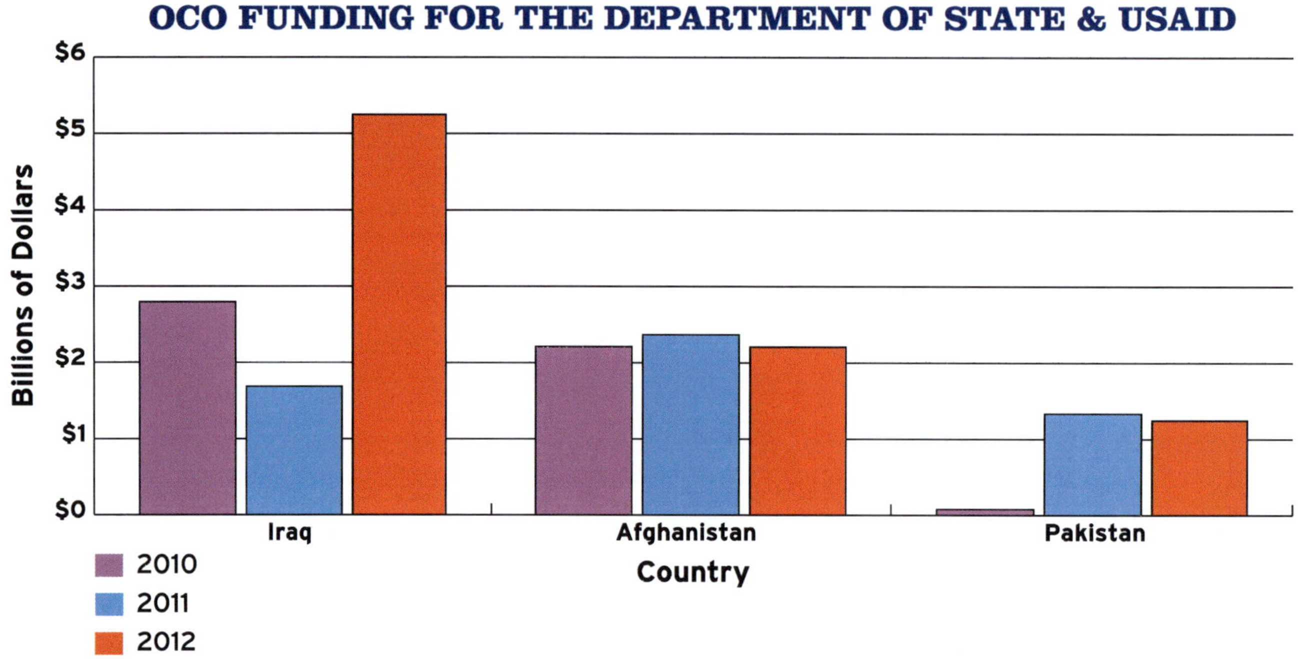

FIGURE 37 SOURCE: Budget of the U.S. Government FY 2012, http://whitehouse.gov/sites/default/files/omb/budget/fy2012/assets/overseas.pdf.

ISSUES TO CONSIDER

These numbers reveal a wealth of information about American priorities in Afghanistan and Iraq. DoD's budget request for FY 2013 included $85.6 billion for Operation Enduring Freedom ($20 billion less than the FY 2012 budget) and a mere $2.9 billion for Operation New Dawn (down $7 billion from FY 2012). This is accompanied by a further drawdown to 68,000 troops in Afghanistan. Operations costs decrease accordingly, as does Equipment Reset; funding for the ANSF is halved, likely because force strength goals for both the Afghan National Army and Afghan National Police are projected to be reached by the end of 2012.[112] It nonetheless remains important to question the efficiency of ANSF training and equipping funds. Multiple investigations have uncovered wasteful allocations and problems with corruption and weak institutions, which take on greater weight as Afghan security forces take over control from American armed forces.[113]

Nor does the question of corruption and institutional frailty pertain solely to the issue of the Afghan National Security Forces. Transparency International's annual Corruptions Perceptions Index, a composite index drawing

111 "Overseas Contingency Operations," Budget of the U.S. Government FY 2012, http://m.whitehouse.gov/sites/default/files/omb/budget/fy2012/assets/overseas.pdf.
112 "Overview: United States Department of Defense Fiscal Year 2013 Budget Request," U.S. Department of Defense, February 2012, http://comptroller.defense.gov/defbudget/fy2013/FY2013_Budget_Request_Overview_Book.pdf.
113 For example, see Greg Bruno, "Afghanistan's National Security Forces," Council on Foreign Relations, August 19, 2010, http://www.cfr.org/afghanistan/afghanistans-national-security-forces/p19122.

on 14 expert opinion surveys, ranked Iraq 175 out of 183 surveyed countries in transparency and perceived lack of corruption, a ranking that has not budged since 2007.[114]

Allan Stam, a professor of political science at the University of Michigan, noted that a "culture of corruption" exists among contractors in Iraq, a culture that incentivizes cutting corners and maximizing profits at the expense of satisfactorily completing projects. Finished projects can thus be useless or near-useless, lacking crucial elements necessary to their function and requiring significant further spending to render them functional.

Stam further questioned whether the sheer amount of money pumped into the economies of Iraq and Afghanistan through a combination of aid and war spending exceeded the potentials of these relatively small economies, resulting in wasteful "run-off."[115]

Going forward, America will have to consider how best to exercise soft power in both theaters without maintaining costly military resources, whether that necessitates diplomatic support through the Department of State or economic development through USAID. The U.S. must consider efficient ways to maintain a strategic presence in the Middle East and Central Asia without jeopardizing American relations abroad or overly burdening the American taxpayer.

These priorities, along with the ongoing issues of how to combat corruption and optimize foreign aid, are among the ones that should drive debate over funding in Iraq and Afghanistan in the years to come.

★

114 "Iraq Index: Tracking Variables of Reconstruction and Security in Iraq," Brookings Institution, July 2012, http://www.brookings.edu/about/centers/saban/~/media/Centers/saban/iraq%20index/index201207.pdf.

115 Allan Stam, interview by author, July 11, 2012. Professor Stam cited the investigative and legislative work on corruption and spending in Iraq spearheaded by Rep. Peter Welch (D-VT).

by Elsa Kania

OBAMA'S PIVOT ON TRADE

Trade is a critical element of the U.S. economy and has continuously grown as a percentage of GDP. From a purely economic perspective, global free trade is generally accepted as maximizing aggregate economic welfare. When each country sticks to its comparative advantage, net economic benefit increases. For producers, free trade provides access to new markets across the globe; consumers appreciate cheap and varied goods. According to the Bureau of Economic Analysis at the U.S. Department of Commerce, exports were 12 percent of U.S. GDP and imports were 18 percent of GDP for the first quarter of 2012.[116] According to the Office of the U.S. Trade Representative, exports also provided approximately 9.7 million jobs to American workers in 2011.[117]

EXPORTS AND IMPORTS, 2010 - 2012

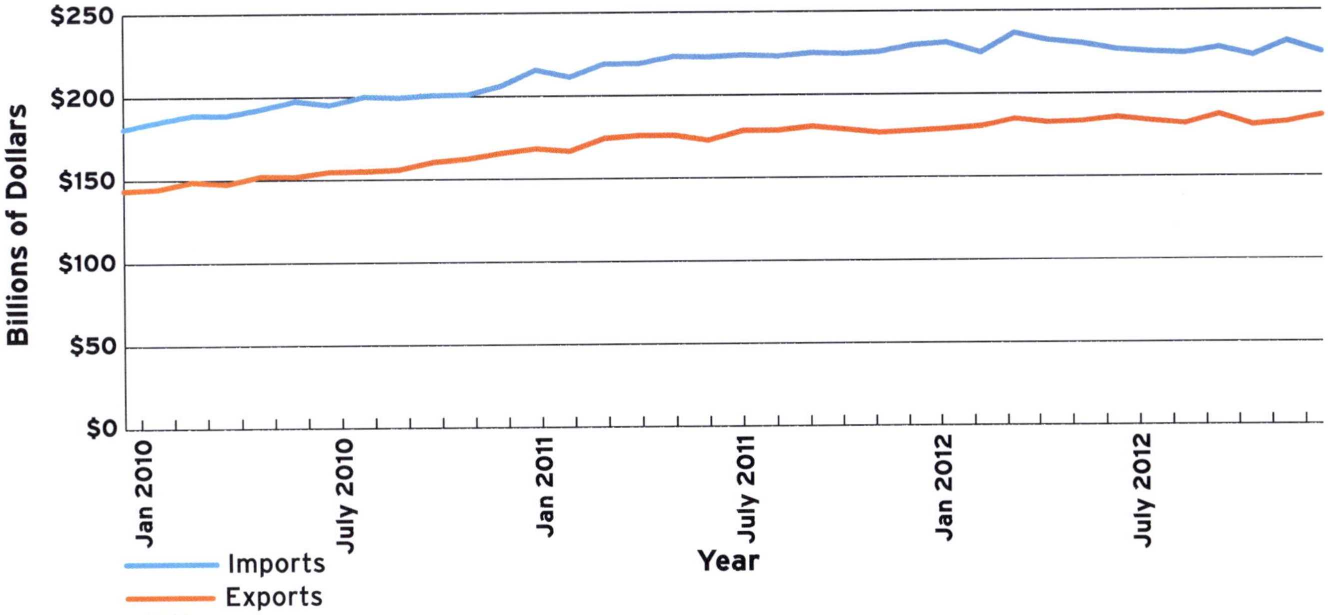

FIGURE 38 SOURCE: U.S. Census Bureau, http://www.census.gov/foreign-trade/data/index.html and http://www.census.gov/foreign-trade/Press-Release/current_press_release/ft900xls.zip.

116 "GDP and the Economy: Second Estimates for the First Quarter of 2012," Bureau of Economic Analysis, U.S. Department of Commerce, June 2012, http://www.bea.gov/scb/pdf/2012/06%20June/0612_gdpecon.pdf.

117 "Benefits of Trade," Office of the U.S. Trade Representative, http://www.ustr.gov/about-us/benefits-trade/.

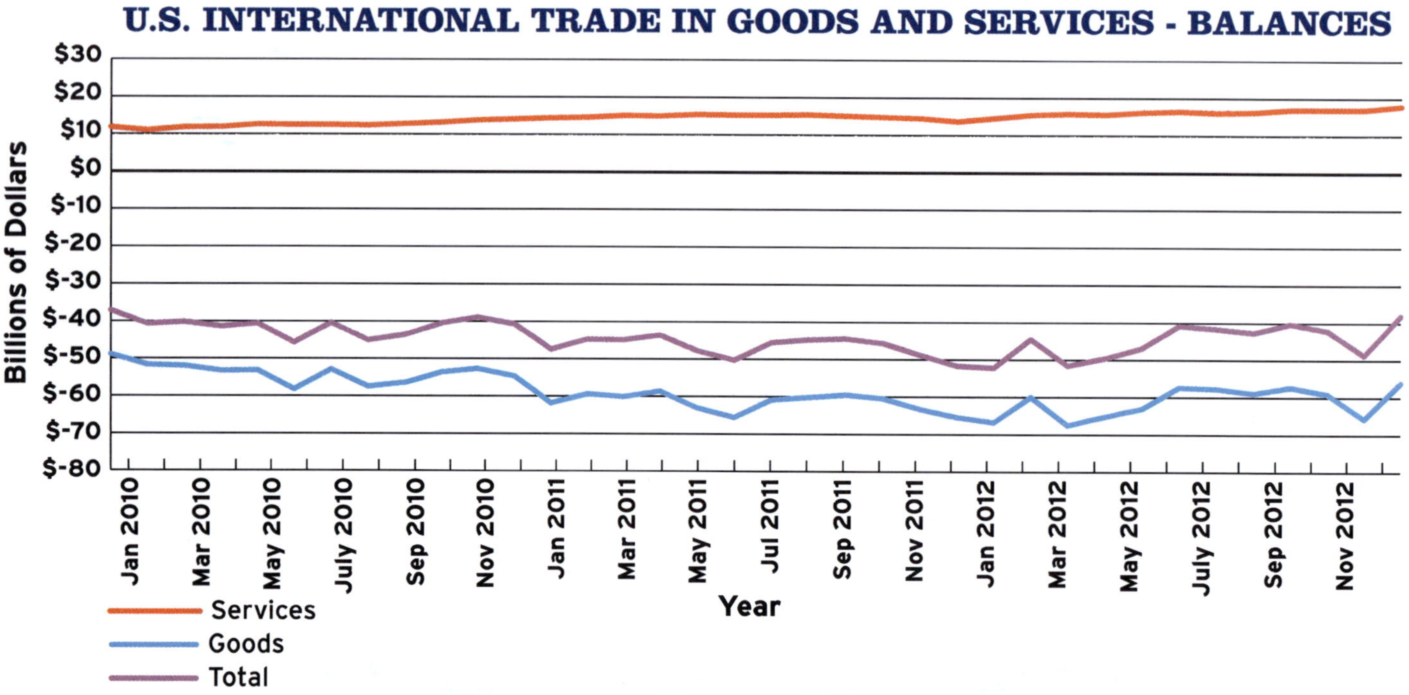

FIGURE 39 SOURCE: U.S. Census Bureau, http://www.census.gov/foreign-trade/data/index.html and http://www.census.gov/foreign-trade/Press-Release/current_press_release/ft900xls.zip.

These favorable trends have dovetailed with a greater focus on trade policy by President Obama, with special attention to the full importance of trade in America's economic recovery. In his 2010 State of the Union address, Obama announced an ambitious goal: "We will double our exports over the next five years, an increase that will support two million jobs in America."[118] To accomplish this objective—initially criticized by some as unfeasible—he created the National Export Initiative, which, if successful, will entail an increase in American exports from $1.57 trillion in 2009 to $3.14 trillion in 2015.[119]

Some, however, argue that Obama's ostensible interest in trade has not translated into political progress. In recent years, "although lip service has been paid to boosting U.S. exports, trade policy accomplishments have been modest," according to Robert Lawrence, a professor at the Harvard Kennedy School and a member of President Clinton's Council of Economic Advisers.[120]

Despite these criticisms, though, this goal of increased trade now seems to be in reach. For the United States, the recent surge of exports has been a rare bright spot within an otherwise bleak economic outlook. In 2011, the value of U.S. exports of goods and services was $2.1 trillion, or 14 percent of GDP. But in 2012, the value in exports reached $2.2 trillion, and the trade balance was not as negative as it was in 2011. Manufacturing has particularly been successful, with an increase in exports as U.S. products have become more competitive in international markets.[121] Such success conveys the value of free trade to U.S. economic recovery.

118 Barack Obama, "State of the Union Address," The White House, January 27, 2010, http://www.whitehouse.gov/the-press-office/remarks-president-state-union-address.
119 Sabina Dewan, "Making U.S. Exports Work for Job Creation," Center for American Progress, January 11, 2012, http://www.americanprogress.org/issues/2012/01/exports_job_creation.html.
120 Robert Lawrence, "How Can Trade Policy Help America Compete?" Harvard Business School, November 2011, http://www.hks.harvard.edu/fs/rlawrence/Lawrence%20Trade%20PolicyHBS.pdf.
121 "Exporting Is Good for Your Bottom Line," International Trade Administration, http://trade.gov/cs/factsheet.asp.

FIGURE 40

SOURCE: U.S. Census Bureau, http://www.census.gov/foreign-trade/data/index.html and http://www.census.gov/foreign-trade/Press-Release/current_press_release/ft900xls.zip.

WHY—AND WHY NOT—FREE TRADE?

Nonetheless, trade policy, long a contentious political issue marked by deep partisan divisions, has been a source of controversy for the Obama administration. According to some within his own party, President Obama has pursued free trade agreements at the expense of American workers and without receiving adequate concessions from trading partners. Republicans, on the other hand, often accuse Obama of being too passive in the pursuit of free trade agreements (FTAs), considered by some to be an arena for geopolitical competition.

THE AMERICAN APPROACH

In general, U.S. trade policy could be characterized in terms of what Lawrence described as a "multi-track approach," with simultaneous efforts towards not only multilateral arrangements through World Trade Organization agreements but also bilateral free trade agreements with trading partners.[122] Characteristically, U.S. trade policy has tended to incorporate reciprocity and take advantage of political or strategic linkages.

According to the U.S. Department of Commerce's International Trade Administration, the United States has enacted free trade agreements with twenty countries, ranging from Canada to Singapore.[123] In negotiating free trade agreements, the United States is able to use the leverage provided by its large market size. Such agreements typically follow what Lawrence described as a "template" with a standardized set of conditions.[124] However, FTAs themselves have been the subject of controversy and are seen by some as "building blocks" that contribute to a

122 Robert Lawrence, interview by author, 2012.
123 For more information, see the International Trade Administration's page "Concluded Trade Agreements," http://www.trade.gov/mas/ian/tradeagreements/fta/tg_ian_002401.asp.
124 Robert Lawrence, interview by author, 2012.

more open global economic order but by others as "stumbling blocks" that create the potential for global markets to fragment regionally.

In bilateral and multilateral efforts alike, Obama initially placed less emphasis on trade policies than previous presidents did. Not until October 2011 did Congress approve trade agreements with South Korea, Colombia, and Panama that had been first finalized under the Bush administration in 2007.[125]

By contrast, under President Bush, the U.S. passed an unprecedented number of bilateral trade agreements, expanding the total from three to fourteen as well as crafting the Dominican Republic–Central America Free Trade Agreement (CAFTA-DR).

The underlying partisan gridlock that had delayed the passage of these FTAs was evident in the voting patterns. All 22 votes against the Panama FTA and all 15 votes against the South Korea FTA came from Democrats, and only two Republicans joined with 31 Democrats in opposing the FTA with Colombia.[126]

Even as President Obama hailed the FTAs as "a major win for American workers and businesses," another Democrat from Illinois condemned the South Korea FTA as a "bad deal for American workers." The success of these agreements required the renewal of the Trade Adjustment Assistance (TAA) program to help the "losers" from these deals (i.e., workers who might find their jobs in jeopardy). Although the full impact of these trade deals has yet to be felt, estimates at the time anticipated an additional $13 billion in exports to South Korea.[127]

THE "PIVOT" ON TRADE

Beyond FTAs, President Obama has taken an increasingly active approach towards trade issues. For example, he established the Interagency Trade Enforcement Center to investigate and address possible violations of international trade agreements.[128] Meanwhile, the Trans-Pacific Partnership, a broad-based free trade agreement among Pacific nations, is reaching a critical stage in negotiations and could provide further opportunities for economic recovery while complementing strategic objectives. A report by the Congressional Research Service described this agreement as "one vehicle that could be used to shape the U.S. agenda with the region."[129]

★

125 Robert Lawrence, "How Can Trade Policy Help America Compete?" Harvard Business School, November 2011, http://www.hks.harvard.edu/fs/rlawrence/Lawrence%20Trade%20PolicyHBS.pdf.

126 Jennifer Rubin, "Congress Passes Free Trade Deals," *The Washington Post*, October 13, 2011, http://www.washingtonpost.com/blogs/right-turn/post/congress-passes-free-trade-deals/2011/03/29/gIQAdI6BhL_blog.html.

127 Elizabeth Williamson and Tom Barkely, "Congress Approves Trade Pacts," *Wall Street Journal*, October 13, 2011, http://online.wsj.com/article/SB10001424052970204002304576627091244722676.html.

128 Carol E. Lee and Sudeep Reddy, "Obama Panel To Watch Beijing," *Wall Street Journal*, January 10, 2012, http://online.wsj.com/article/SB10001424052970203436904577151273759279432.html.

129 Ian F. Fergusson and Bruce Vaughn, "The Trans-Pacific Partnership Agreement," Congressional Research Service, June 25, 2010, http://fpc.state.gov/documents/organization/145583.pdf.

by Marina Bolotnikova

Like many other programs, federal education funding expanded from a virtually nonexistent service to a seemingly indispensable one over the course of the twentieth century. Historically, state and local governments have provided almost all education funding. It was not until 1965, when Title I of the Elementary and Secondary Education Act (ESEA) was passed under President Lyndon B. Johnson, that the federal government became a significant player in education financing.

Title I, a component of the Johnson administration's civil rights project that aimed to improve educational opportunities for underserved students, still remains "the most important federal education program by far," said John Chubb, interim CEO of Education Sector, a non-profit education think tank.[130] Today, Title I grants alone make up 21 percent of the budget of the U.S. Department of Education.[131] Title I typifies the federal government's philosophy on education finance: school funding is primarily the responsibility of state and local governments, and the federal government intervenes to correct inequalities in access to education within and among states.

More recently, the federal government has assumed additional roles in financing education. The government has begun holding schools accountable for improvements in education and even promoting specific educational policies, such as charter schools. These programs aim to improve equitable access to education and may thus be interpreted as generous extensions of the Johnson administration's initial provision of blanket funds to needy school districts under Title I. But strictly speaking, though federal education finance has expanded enormously in the last half century (see Figure 43), the overwhelming majority of K-12 funding is still dispensed by state and local governments. Nationally, federal funding makes up less than 10 percent of school funding.[132] Likewise, though the federal government's total FY 2012 budget for education and related programs totaled a staggering $170 billion, it represented a small fraction of the total federal budget.

Today, federal education funding encompasses a tremendous variety of programs funded not only by the U.S. Department of Education but also by the U.S. Departments of Agriculture, of Health and Human Services, and of Labor.[133] The breadth and complexity of federal education finance is staggering; many of the government's miscellaneous education funding programs seem to defy easy interpretation and classification. Bearing this in mind, it is first necessary to consider where federal spending on education goes.

K-12 SPENDING

About two-thirds of the overall federal budget is made up of what is known as mandatory spending, which is money that the federal government is required to spend each year. The remaining one-third of federal spending is made up of discretionary spending, which is the money that the government is authorized to spend only in the current fiscal year through the annual congressional appropriations process. Most federal education funding comes from discretionary spending.[134]

130 John Chubb, interview by author, June 4, 2012.
131 "Education in the Federal Budget," New America Foundation, March 22, 2012, http://febp.newamerica.net/background-analysis/education-federal-budget.
132 "Federal, State, and Local K-12 School Finance Overview," New America Foundation, December 13, 2012, http://febp.newamerica.net/background-analysis/school-finance.
133 "Education in the Federal Budget," New America Foundation, March 22, 2012, http://febp.newamerica.net/background-analysis/education-federal-budget.
134 "Budget of the U.S. Government: Analytical Perspectives," Office of Management and Budget, February 13, 2012, http://www.gpo.gov/fdsys/pkg/BUDGET-2013-PER/pdf/BUDGET-2013-PER.pdf.

FEDERAL K - 12 SPENDING, FY 2012 (billions of dollars)

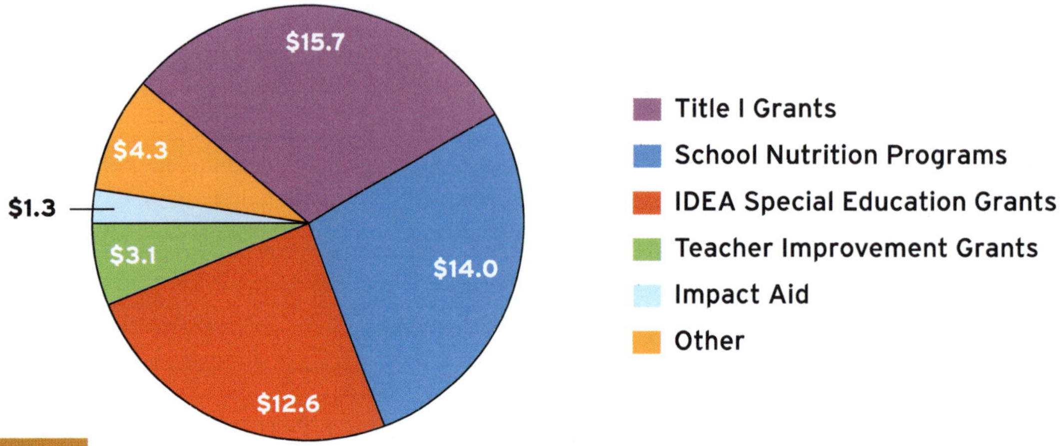

FIGURE 41

Elementary and secondary education received $51 billion in the FY 2012 budget. Much of this funding went to two large programs: No Child Left Behind (NCLB) Title I grants and Individuals with Disabilities Education Act (IDEA) special education grants. Title I of the Elementary and Secondary Education Act of 1965, reauthorized by the Bush administration's No Child Left Behind Act in 2001, remains the most significant source of federal funding for K-12 education. In FY 2012, $15.7 billion in Title I grants were distributed to school districts.

Importantly, Title I funds are distributed to districts according to a complex formula that estimates local need.[135] Districts with higher proportions of students living below the federal poverty level receive relatively more Title I funds than districts with wealthier students. This explains in large part why federal funding makes up different proportions of the education budgets of different states. For example, federal funds constitute 16.4 percent of the education budget of South Dakota, while the federal share of education funding in New Jersey is just 4.1 percent. But despite these disparities, over half of school districts receive some Title I funding.

A total of $12.6 billion in IDEA special education grants, the second-largest federal K-12 funding program, was distributed in FY 2012 to improve special education programs. Unlike Title I grants, which are distributed to school districts, IDEA grants are distributed to states because states are required by law to provide students with disabilities an adequate education.[136]

Other notable sources of federal education finance include the Impact Aid programs,[137] Improving Teacher Quality state grants,[138] and English Language Acquisition state grants,[139] all of which are stipulated by NCLB. Impact Aid grants provided $1.29 billion in FY 2012 to school districts with a limited availability of local funding for education due to "federal activities."[140] Federally owned and Native American land, for example, are not subject to property taxes, which account for a significant proportion of local school funding, and thus receive Impact Aid.[141]

135 Jennifer Cohen Kabaker, "Congress Gearing Up for a Title I Formula Fight," New America Foundation, August 9, 2011, http://edmoney.newamerica.net/node/56115.
136 "Federal, State, and Local K-12 School Finance Overview," New America Foundation, December 13, 2012, http://febp.newamerica.net/background-analysis/school-finance.
137 "About Impact Aid," U.S. Department of Education, August 27, 2008, http://www2.ed.gov/about/offices/list/oese/impactaid/whatisia.html.
138 "Improving Teacher Quality State Grants," U.S. Department of Education, November 13, 2009, http://www2.ed.gov/programs/teacherqual/index.html.
139 "English Language Acquisition State Grants," U.S. Department of Education, August 3, 2011, http://www2.ed.gov/programs/sfgp/index.html.
140 "Federal, State, and Local K-12 School Finance Overview," New America Foundation, December 13, 2012, http://febp.newamerica.net/background-analysis/school-finance.
141 Senate Report 112-84, Library of Congress, September 22, 2011, http://www.gpo.gov/fdsys/pkg/CRPT-112srpt84/pdf/CRPT-112srpt84.pdf.

Improving Teacher Quality state grants provided $2.5 billion to states in FY 2012 to improve teacher quality in public schools, and the English Language Acquisition grant program distributed $732 million to schools to improve English acquisition for students with limited proficiency in English.[142]

THE NO CHILD LEFT BEHIND CONTROVERSY

The aim of both ESEA and the No Child Left Behind Act is to improve educational opportunities for underserved students. In this sense, NCLB is similar in spirit to its predecessor. But NCLB also represents an important departure from earlier forms of federal education funding. Whereas ESEA awarded blanket funds to school districts in order to provide educational opportunities to low-income students, NCLB also seeks to hold schools accountable for improvements in education. NCLB marks "the first time that the federal government asked schools to show academic outcomes as a condition for receiving funds," said Jennifer Cohen, an education policy expert who has worked at the New America Foundation and the Urban Institute.[143]

Under NCLB, schools that receive Title I funding are required to reach 100 percent student competence in grade-level reading and math by 2014. In order to reach this lofty goal, schools are expected to make Adequate Yearly Progress (AYP). AYP is state defined and usually amounts to an increase in the number of students performing at grade-level by a few percentage points. Schools that do not meet AYP are deemed schools "in need of improvement" and become subject to a variety of disciplinary measures depending on the number of years for which they have fallen short of their goal. For example, if a school fails to meet AYP two years in a row, parents are entitled to transfer their children to a school that is not "in need of improvement" at no charge. Schools that fail to meet AYP six years in a row are required to restructure their governance.[144]

Much ink has been spilled about the efficacy of NCLB, and many people take issue with the practical shortcomings of the program. "The government does not have a good track record for evaluating the efficacy of education finance," said John Chubb, the interim CEO of Education Sector.[145]

Jennifer Cohen agreed. "Currently, the government only measures the degree to which Title I is meeting its goals," said Cohen, "and the goal of Title I is only to distribute funds and services to low-income students. But the real question is how effective the funds are at improving achievement."[146]

As far as improving achievement is concerned, Cohen said that NCLB falls short in a number of important ways. The comparability provision of NCLB requires states to provide equal pay to teachers in all districts, with the goal of ensuring that schools in both high- and low-income communities are able to attract talented teachers. But this seemingly powerful provision, Cohen said, is not very effective because schools still pay teachers with more experience and qualifications comparably higher salaries. And because higher-quality teachers with the most experience tend to work in schools serving high-income communities, some believe that the comparability provision may actually undermine the goal of Title I.[147]

142 "Federal, State, and Local K-12 School Finance Overview," New America Foundation, December 13, 2012, http://febp.newamerica.net/background-analysis/school-finance.
143 Jennifer Cohen, interview by author, June 15, 2012.
144 "No Child Left Behind (NCLB) Requirements for Schools," GreatSchools, http://www.greatschools.org/definitions/nclb/nclb.html.
145 John Chubb, interview by author, June 4, 2012.
146 "Improving Teacher Quality State Grants," U.S. Department of Education, November 13, 2009, http://www2.ed.gov/programs/teacherqual/index.html.
147 Jennifer Cohen Kabaker, "Congress Gearing Up for a Title I Formula Fight," New America Foundation, August 9, 2011, http://edmoney.newamerica.net/node/56115.

Cohen and other experts also believe that the government's measure of AYP is ineffective. Currently, students in Title I schools are divided into demographic subcategories, such as White, Hispanic, and special education. If one of these subgroups fails to meet AYP in one subject in a particular year, the entire school is considered to have failed. What is more, schools are not given credit for partial improvement. This means that if a school's AYP goal for a particular year is a 3.0 percent improvement in performance, a 2.0 percent increase will be treated no differently from no increase at all. Cohen described this as "a very un-nuanced accountability system."[148]

Still others criticize the philosophical grounds of NCLB. Some experts and policymakers argue that local officials should make decisions about education policy. The federal government, they assert, may not be aware of the particularities and complex needs of local communities. "The federal government wants to give money with a lot of strings attached," said Michael Kirst, president of the California State Board of Education. But others believe that federal regulations are necessary to ensure that Title I funds are used in accordance with their purpose: to create educational opportunities for underserved demographics.[149]

Finally, some people criticize NCLB for penalizing schools that do not meet AYP, arguing that this approach casts underperforming schools as delinquent and requires them to implement corrective measures that may not address the root of school underperformance.[150]

EDUCATION REFORM IN THE OBAMA ERA

President Obama has introduced a number of funding programs that not only stipulate improvements in school performance as a condition for continued funding but also reward specific educational policies. In this way, the Obama administration's approach to education finance may be interpreted as a continuation of the precedent set by the Bush administration. The current administration's most prominent education funding program, Race to the Top (RTTT), typifies this approach. In 2009, the President issued an economic stimulus package that included $4.5 billion for RTTT. A portion of this money will be made available through appropriations in Congress each year until the funding runs out.[151]

RTTT invites states and school districts to compete for funding by implementing reforms, such as evaluating teachers and principals based on performance, promoting charter schools, and reforming low-achieving schools.[152] In 2011, nine states were awarded a total of $500 million to fund early education programs.[153] In FY 2012, the federal government was projected to award a total of $400 million to school districts, not states, to implement education reforms. Individual awards were to range from $15 million to $25 million, depending on the number of students in the district.[154]

RTTT, like NCLB, is often the subject of national debate. Some note that the competition has led to positive reforms in many states; others argue that RTTT promotes educational policies that the current administration

148 "Improving Teacher Quality State Grants," U.S. Department of Education, November 13, 2009, http://www2.ed.gov/programs/teacherqual/index.html.
149 Michael Kirst, interview by author, May 29, 2012.
150 Justine S. Hastings and Jeffrey M. Weinstein, "No Child Left Behind: Estimating the Impact on Choices and Student Outcomes," Yale University, March 2007, http://aida.econ.yale.edu/~jh529/papers/Hastings&Weinstein_NCLB.pdf.
151 "Race to the Top Fund," U.S. Department of Education, http://www2.ed.gov/programs/racetothetop/index.html.
152 "Race to the Top Program: Executive Summary," U.S. Department of Education, November 2009, http://www2.ed.gov/programs/racetothetop/executive-summary.pdf.
153 "Nine States Awarded Race to the Top—Early Learning Challenge Grant," The White House, December 16, 2011, http://www.whitehouse.gov/the-press-office/2011/12/16/we-cant-wait-nine-states-awarded-race-top-early-learning-challenge-grant.
154 "District-level Race to the Top to Focus on the Classroom, Provide Tools to Enhance Learning and Serve the Needs of Every Student," U.S. Department of Education, May 22, 2012, http://www.ed.gov/news/press-releases/district-level-race-top-focus-classroom-provide-tools-enhance-learning-and-serve.

favors at the expense of local autonomy. In any case, it is clear that the government's current education finance policy is evidence of an increasing degree of federal involvement in education reform.

HIGHER EDUCATION FUNDING

Increasingly, as higher education has started to become the foundation of a productive American economy and as tuition fees have increased rapidly, the federal government has expanded its higher education grant and loan programs. In FY 2012, $42.5 billion in federal funding was spent on grant programs for higher education. The majority of this money went to the Pell Grant program alone, which distributed $38.2 billion in grants, or about one-third of the budget of the Department of Education, to about 9 million undergraduate students in need (see Table 12). So much money is spent on Pell Grants that they are often excluded from federal education budget summaries because they dwarf other sources of spending.

FEDERAL HIGHER EDUCATION SPENDING, FY 2012 (billions of dollars)

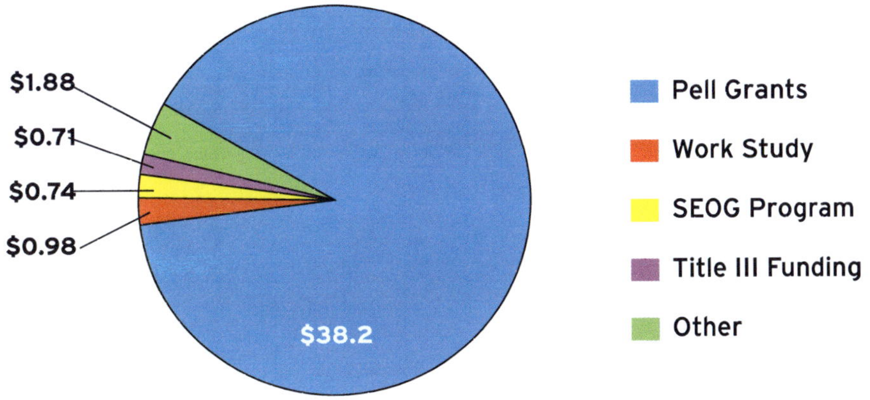

FIGURE 42

Individual Pell Grant awards range from a few hundred dollars to over $5,000, depending on need. Financial need is determined by a formula that compares a student's cost of college attendance with his or her Expected Family Contribution (EFC). If a student's EFC is lower than the value of the maximum Pell Grant, he or she is eligible to receive a grant. Luckily for students, the College Cost Reduction and Access Act of 2007 set aside $33.6 billion in mandatory supplementary funding for the Pell Grant to be spent by 2017. This means that on top of their need-based award, Pell recipients will each be awarded an additional lump sum. As a result, the maximum Pell award in FY 2012 was $5,550: $4,860 in discretionary funding and $690 in mandatory funding stipulated by the College Cost Reduction and Access Act. While discretionary appropriations for the Pell Grant have not risen since 2009 and are not expected to rise for several years, Pell awards have increased and are expected to continue increasing as a result of this legislation. Below is a summary of the sources of funding for Pell Grant awards from 2008 to 2014.

TABLE 12 - PELL GRANT FUNDING AND AWARD LEVEL BY YEAR

	2008	2009	2010	2011	2012	2013	2014
Funding by Source ($ billions)							
Appropriation*	$14.2	$17.3	$17.5	$23.0	$22.8	$21.0	$30.7
Prior years' surplus	--	--	--	--	--	$2.1	--
ARRA funds	--	$12.3	$3.4	--	--	--	--
ARRA mandatory/entitlement funds	--	$0.6	$0.8	--	--	--	--
2010 Student loan reform (one-time funds)	--	--	$10.7	$2.8	--	--	--
2011 year-round grant elimination	--	--	--	$3.2	--	--	--
Budget Control Act	--	--	--	$0.2	$9.8	$7.0	--
2012 Grace period interest subsidy elimination/other	--	--	--	--	$0.6	$0.6	$0.6
Mandatory/entitlement formula	$2.0	$2.1	$4.5	$5.3	$5.3	$5.8	$6.5
Total	**$16.2**	**$32.3**	**$36.9**	**$35.5**	**$38.2**	**$36.4**	**$37.8**
Maximum Grant ($)							
Appropriation	$4,241	$4,860	$4,860	$4,860	$4,860	$4,860**	$4,860**
Mandatory/entitlement	$490	$490	$690	$690	$690	$785**	$865**
Total	**$4,731**	**$5,350**	**$5,550**	**$5,550**	**$5,550**	**$5,645**	**$5,725**

* Appropriations prior to 2013 are current law; figures for 2013 and 2014 reflect estimates of the appropriation needed to fund the grant level shown at the bottom. All other funding sources are currently in law.

** Estimate.

SOURCE: New America Foundation.

TABLE 13 - OTHER HIGHER EDUCATION FUNDING PROGRAMS

Program	Description	Academic Year 2011-2012 Funding
Federal Work-Study Program (FWSP)	Subsidizes employment opportunities for students at their college, university, or outside employer. FWSP funding pays up to half of students' wages.	$977 million
Supplemental Educational Opportunity Grants (SEOG)	Distributes need-based funds for student grants directly to colleges and universities.	$735 million
Title III Grants	Distributes grants to colleges and universities that serve low-income and minority groups, such as historically black colleges and universities. These funds are used at the discretion of each institution.	$707 million

SOURCE: "Other Federal Higher Education Grant Programs," New America Foundation, March 26, 2012, http://febp.newamerica.net/background-analysis/federal-higher-education-grant-programs.

THE FUTURE OF EDUCATION SPENDING

Many of the contentious topics discussed above are expected to shape the national debate on education policy in the coming years. Anne Hyslop, a policy analyst at Education Sector, noted that the federal government will soon have to address its enormous increases in education expenditures, especially on higher education. For instance, the Pell Grant program, Hyslop said, "is eating up a larger portion of education spending each year."[155] As state budgets remain stagnant, it seems that the federal government will have to sustain its current levels of spending on education, an arrangement that will prove challenging after stimulus funding runs out.

As the government plays an increasingly large role in financing schools and institutions of higher learning, it faces the dual tasks of not only implementing policy in a way that respects local needs but also developing standards of evaluation that are fair, nuanced, and rigorous. While the federal government has played an increasingly significant role in education for nearly half a century, it has yet to develop a well-defined platform to direct its involvement in education policy in the future.

FEDERAL EDUCATION SPENDING, 1962 - 2012 (real)

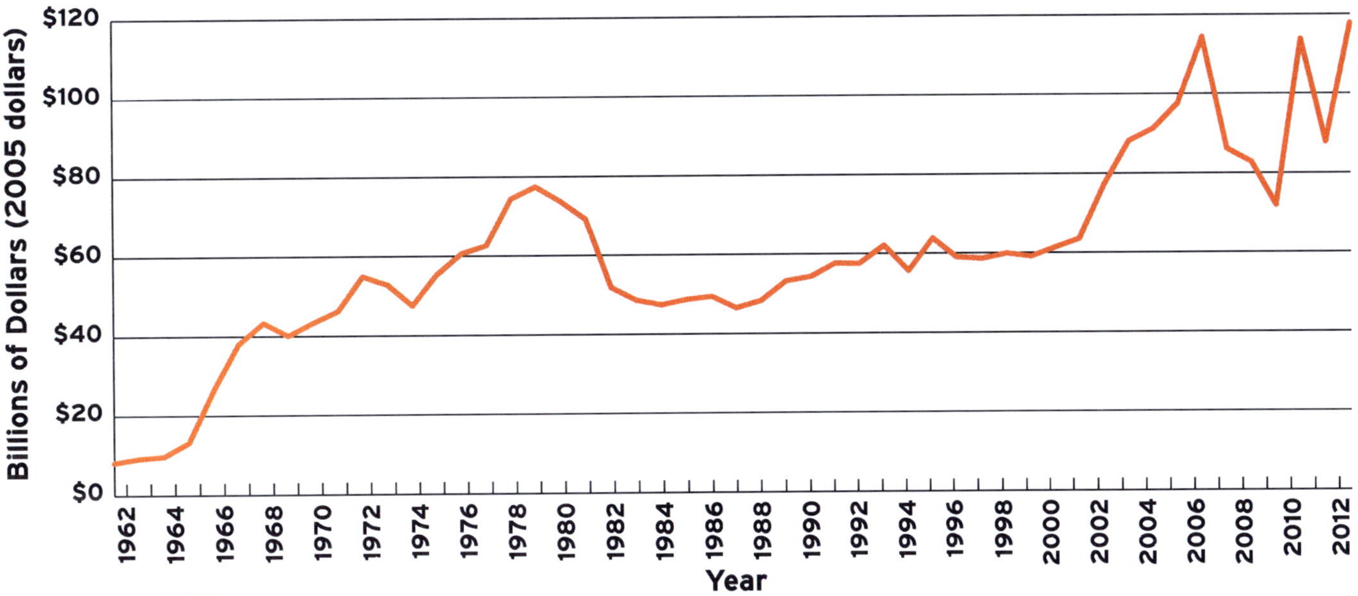

FIGURE 43

SOURCE: Budget of the U.S. Government FY 2013, http://www.gpo.gov/fdsys/pkg/BUDGET-2013-TAB/xls/BUDGET-2013-TAB-3-2.xls.

155 Anne Hyslop, e-mail message to author, June 16, 2012.

COMPOSITION OF FEDERAL EDUCATION SPENDING, 1962 - 2012

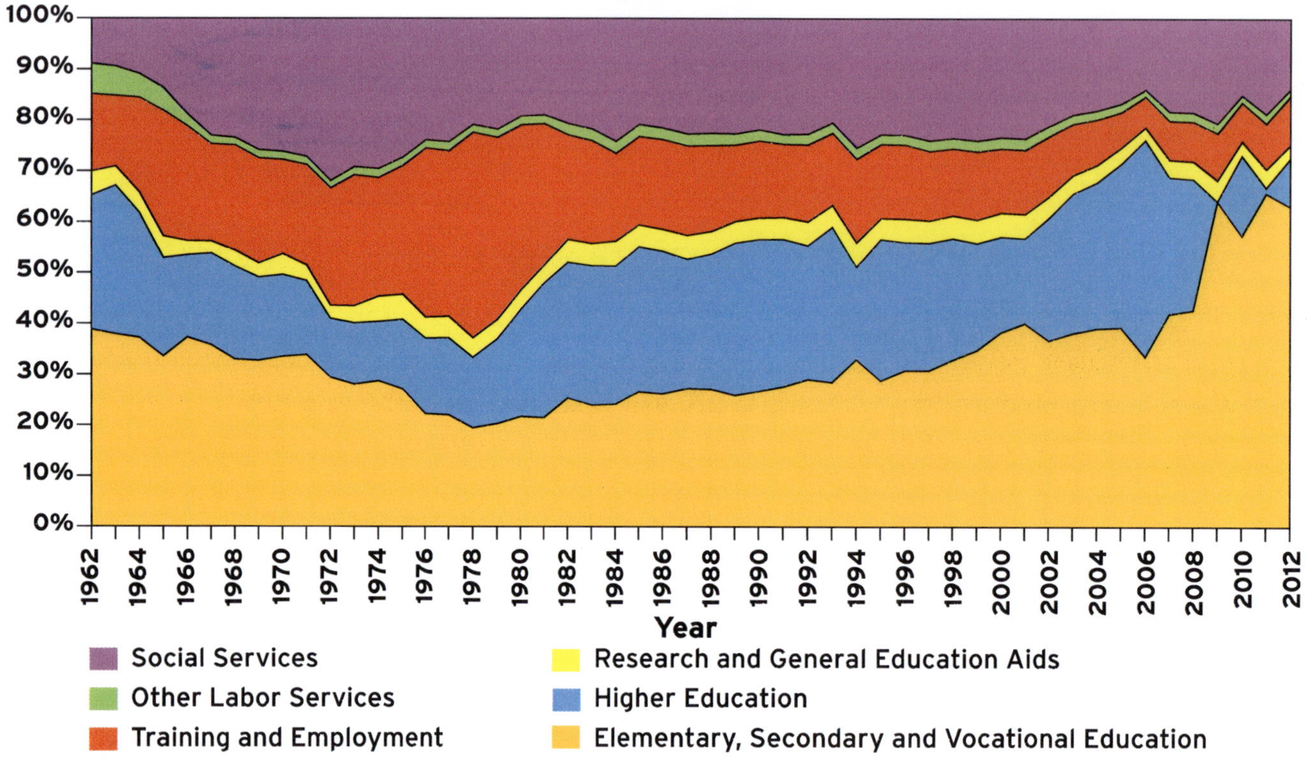

FIGURE 44 SOURCE: Budget of the U.S. Government FY 2013, http://www.gpo.gov/fdsys/pkg/BUDGET-2013-TAB/xls/BUDGET-2013-TAB-3-2.xls.

★

EDUCATION, SCIENCE, & TECHNOLOGY: SCIENCE

by Cassandra Thomson

Understanding how the federal government funds basic scientific research and technological development requires unpacking the complex "science" spending function in the federal budget. Though 64 percent of overall research and development funding is provided by private industry in America, the federal government provides significant grants to the scientific community through public institutions.[156] Considering that the suspected discovery of the Higgs-Boson particle in July 2012 was estimated to cost over $13.25 billion, it is clear that science is an area in which large amounts of money have become necessary for most innovation and research.[157]

Analyzing the science budget also requires recognition of the complexity of funding sources within the federal budget itself. There is no central scientific agency that allocates funds to various endeavors, but rather a collection of departments that are each accorded varying amounts. The most well known of these agencies include the Department of Energy (DoE), National Aeronautics and Space Administration (NASA), National Institutes of Health (NIH), and National Science Foundation (NSF).

To make sense of this network of scientific agencies and the current funding situation, it is helpful to analyze the science budget according to several sectors: general science, space, and technology; energy and alternative energy sources; natural resources and the environment; and health research.

SCIENCE SPENDING, 1962 - 2012 (real)

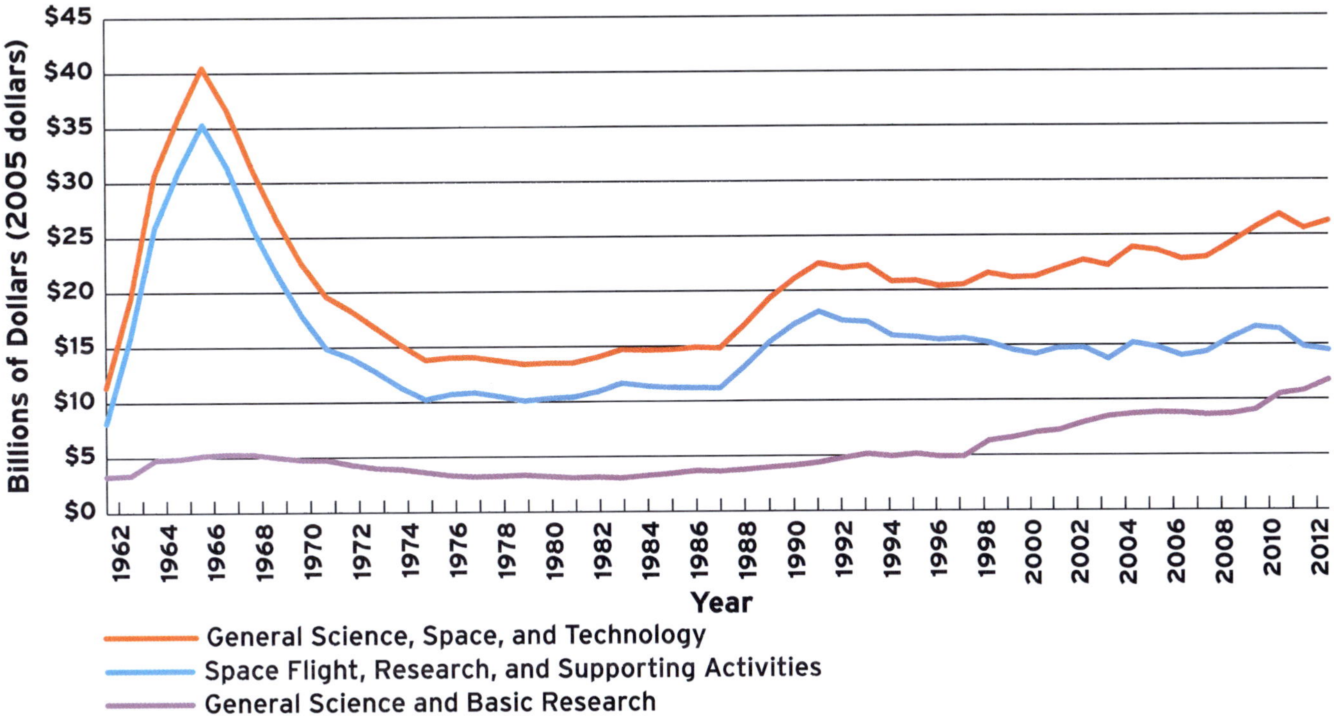

FIGURE 45

SOURCE: Budget of the U.S. Government FY 2013, http://www.gpo.gov/fdsys/pkg/BUDGET-2013-TAB/xls/BUDGET-2013-TAB-3-2.xls.

156 Martin Grueber, "2012 Global R&D Funding Forecast: Stable Growth of U.S. R&D," *R&D Magazine*, December 16, 2011, http://www.rdmag.com/Featured-Articles/2011/12/2012-Global-RD-Funding-Forecast-Stable-Growth-Of-US-RD/.

157 Alex Knapp, "How Much Does It Cost to Find a Higgs Boson?" *Forbes*, July 5, 2012, http://www.forbes.com/sites/alexknapp/2012/07/05/how-much-does-it-cost-to-find-a-higgs-boson/.

GENERAL SCIENCE, SPACE, AND TECHNOLOGY

Though spending on scientific research is harder to define than spending on national defense or health care, even the most inclusive domain of the federal science budget—the general science, space, and technology domain—can be categorized based on several related funding agencies.

National Science Foundation (NSF)

Jurisdiction: Issues competitive, limited-term grants to the research community, funding about 10,000 proposals out of 40,000 received annually.

Current Funding: Received $6.694 billion in FY 2012 and $6.738 billion in FY 2011.

History: Has provided funding for both research and educational efforts in non-biomedical disciplines since its formation in 1950.

Website: http://www.nsf.gov/

The President's 2009 decision to double funding for the NSF did not hold due to the recession, but the fears that had surfaced over threats by House Republicans to cut research funding during the 2012 budget deliberations were not realized, either.[158] In fact, general non-space science overall experienced an increase in allocated funds in 2012, with a total of $11.838 billion, or an increase of about $203 million from the 2011 budget.

Despite a long series of complaints by NSF Director Subra Suresh about the limited funds for the agency's budget overall, the 2012 year was marked by NSF efforts to "streamline the grants-making process to free up NSF's 1,500 employees for other activities," while also "reduc[ing] the burden on outside scientists who serve as reviewers."[159] Thus, though the final budget did not come near the amount originally requested by President Obama, the NSF made serious improvements: not only enhancing efficiency by informally stretching the budget but also gaining more freedom to redistribute particular funds among the branches of the NSF.

U.S. Department of Energy, Office of Science

Jurisdiction: Supports general science research in biological, environmental, and computational sciences, with alternative branches sustaining energy research. Allocations are dispersed among ten national labs, including Ames, Argonne, and Fermi, which carry out publicly and nationally purposeful projects ill-suited for the private sector.

Current Funding: Encountered only a minimal decrease in FY 2012 to $4.874 billion from $4.897 billion in FY 2011.

History: With its origins in the World War II Manhattan Project and the race to develop the atomic bomb, the Department of Energy was formally established in 1977.

Website: http://science.energy.gov/

158 Brian Vastag, "NASA and National Science Foundation Are Spared from Big Budget Cuts," *The Washington Post*, November 21, 2011, http://www.washingtonpost.com/national/health-science/nasa-and-national-science-foundation-are-spared-from-big-budget-cuts/2011/11/16/gIQAz7FwhN_story.html.

159 Jeffrey Mervis, "NSF Tops Research Agencies with a $340-Million Boost," *Science Insider*, February 14, 2012, http://news.sciencemag.org/scienceinsider/2012/02/nsf-tops-research-agencies-with.html.

Most divisions in the DoE's Office of Science kept largely stable budgets in FY 2012.[160] Despite the lack of funding increases, most of the recipients have declared gratitude rather than disappointment. "Even staying flat when a lot of other programs are getting cut is relatively good news," said Thom Mason, director of Oak Ridge National Laboratory, in an interview with Science Insider, the blog of renowned scientific publication *Science*.

National Aeronautics and Space Administration (NASA)

Jurisdiction: Administers the U.S. civilian space program in addition to aerospace and aeronautics research.

Current Funding: $17.2 billion in FY 2012, a $700 million decrease from FY 2011.

History: Created in 1958 to respond to pressures of security and national defense surrounding the Cold War.

Website: http://www.nasa.gov/

Cuts to the NASA budget constituted one of the largest recent losses for science funding, a 3.5 percent decrease for FY 2012. Surprisingly, though, NASA has mostly kept its ground despite the heavy losses experienced earlier in this decade.[161] As Kevin Marvel, executive officer of the American Astronomical Society, said, "compared to where we could have been, we are in a good place for 2012."[162]

The most serious losses were in the space operations department. Among the casualties were the International Space Station and the space shuttle, which conducted its last mission in July 2011. All major science initiatives were kept, however, and received an overall $155 million increase above the 2011 level. Among science initiatives, funds will be redirected to the James Webb Space Telescope (JWST). This is the first step in a five-year, $8.8 billion endeavor to build and operate the telescope. Many other programs have been delayed to ensure sufficient funding for a 2018 launch.[163]

Summary

In total, the general science, space, and technology portion of the federal government's science budget received $29.1 billion in funding (excluding the education programs), a slight decrease from FY 2011.[164] The reason for this relatively stable budget in this troubled economy may be due to efforts for economic recovery. The NSF, for example, is the main funding source for "clean energy and climate science, advanced manufacturing and cybersecurity, as well as improving science and math education," all of which are now being cited as among the most promising prospects for economic resurgence.[165] The FY 2012 budget proposal even notes this, stating that "basic research has been America's great strength, creating whole new industries and jobs… Especially as the private sector has reduced the amounts it dedicates to this type of research, it is critical that the Federal Government dedicates funds to it."

160 Adrian Cho, "Senate Budget Bill Holds Energy Department Science Level," *Science Insider*, September 9, 2011, http://news.sciencemag.org/scienceinsider/2011/09/senate-budget-bill-holds-energy.html.
161 Richard M. Jones, "FY 2012 NASA Appropriations Bill Signed into Law," American Institute of Physics, November 18, 2011, http://www.aip.org/fyi/2011/138.html.
162 Ivan Semeniuk, "US Science Agencies Dodge Deep Cuts," *Nature*, November 21, 2011, http://www.nature.com/news/us-science-agencies-dodge-deep-cuts-1.9410.
163 Brian Berger and Dan Leone, "NASA 2012 Budget Funds JWST, Halves Commercial Spaceflight," *Space News International*, November 18, 2011, http://www.spacenews.com/civil/111118-nasa-budget-funds.html.
164 "Analytical Perspectives," Analytical Perspectives. Budget of the U.S. Government FY 2013, http://www.gpo.gov/fdsys/search/pagedetails.action?packageId=BUDGET-2013-PER.
165 Jeffrey Mervis, "NSF Tops Research Agencies with a $340-Million Boost," *Science Insider*, February 14, 2012, http://news.sciencemag.org/scienceinsider/2012/02/nsf-tops-research-agencies-with.html.

In addition, there are subtle warnings in the form of comparisons to international competitors. With budget cuts there could be a withdrawal from research efforts towards new innovations, including discoveries like dark energy that were predicted and discovered by United States scientists but are now being pursued by foreign researchers. Saul Perlmutter of the University of California, Berkeley, put it succinctly: "The danger…is that we will watch the science (and scientists – and good students) move on to other countries and continents, where projects are being begun and completed."[166]

Stability may be seen as a victory now, but the future costs—among others, reduction of early access to new technologies and resources and a deterioration in the long-solid network of American-based scientific researchers—may not be known until future years.

ENERGY AND ALTERNATIVE ENERGY SOURCES

The energy budget begins with the Department of Energy. From its inception in August 1977 with President Carter's Department of Energy Act, the DoE's research has evolved from nuclear weapons development to nuclear cleanup and from research on improving oil use to mass production of alternative, clean-energy sources.[167] Such practices remained part of the DoE's FY 2012 budget appropriations, but alternative energy innovation and mass production through research were not the major goals. Instead, appropriations were used primarily to recover from the fallout of the loan guarantee program and to encourage programs for national security and economic competitiveness.

Justification for science research spending hikes during the recession centered on the economic profitability of new technological investments. However, "the Solyndra scandal" revealed the general ineffectiveness of the DoE's energy loan guarantee program.

Solyndra was a manufacturer of cylindrical thin-film solar cell panels. The company suffered a very public collapse including bankruptcy and the loss of the $535 million guaranteed by the federal government in early September 2011. The company, meant to compete with the Chinese monopoly on the solar panel industry and provide jobs in the U.S., fell to the Chinese producers. (China is said to have offered 20 times more subsidies to its solar companies, making Solyndra's business model unprofitable almost from the beginning.)[168] A subsequent investigation revealed that the government provided loans even as the company's problems became apparent. Furthermore, a string of emails found by *The Washington Post* raised the question of whether funding was based on political considerations.[169]

Indeed, DoE's entire loan program is in trouble. Over $34.7 billion has been guaranteed through loans since 2009, with almost half of this through the Section 1705 loan program that included Solyndra.[170] Despite the formation of 26 projects with approximately $16 billion in total loans, only about 2,378 permanent jobs were created—a

166 Dennis Overbye, "American Physics Dreams Deferred," *The New York Times*, May 21, 2012, http://www.nytimes.com/2012/05/22/science/american-scientists-fear-losing-edge-in-physics.html.

167 "Energy Department," *The Washington Post*, http://www.washingtonpost.com/politics/energy-department/gIQAfo7y4O_topic.html.

168 Yuki Noguchi, "Solyndra Flop May Cost Taxpayers, Embarrass Obama," National Public Radio, September 15, 2011, http://www.npr.org/2011/09/15/140489033/solyndra-flop-may-cost-taxpayers-embarrass-obama.

169 Henry J. Reske and John Bachman, "Rep. Stearns: 'No More Solyndras Act' Protects Taxpayers," Newsmax, July 12, 2012, http://www.newsmax.com/Politics/stearns-solyndra-bill-taxpayers/2012/07/12/id/445120.

170 Veronique De Rugy, "Solyndra Not the Only Questionable Obama Loan to 'Green' Energy," *U.S. News & World Report*, June 19, 2012, http://www.usnews.com/opinion/blogs/economic-intelligence/2012/06/19/solyndra-not-the-only-questionable-obama-loan-to-green-energy.

cost of $6.7 million per job. The loan program's stated goal of encouraging more American jobs was clearly not effectively achieved.

Regardless of whether the basic science investigated under the DoE's programs translated into economic profitability, such reasoning could no longer serve as political justification for why the DoE should invest in promising private companies. The result? A complete lack of funding appropriated to the DoE's energy loans program for FY 2012, and a recall of the $181 million that had not yet been spent.[171]

Comparing the FY 2012 budget to the FY 2011 situation outside of this loan program reveals general funding increases, but not nearly to the degree proposed by the Obama administration. The Office of Energy Efficiency and Renewable Energy (EERE), expecting a large budget increase after the success of FY 2010 and FY 2011, received only small increases in the research and development division. Instead, areas deemed more relevant to national security and economic competitiveness were the winners in this area, resulting in more funding for nuclear energy ($505 million) and for fossil fuel research and development ($81 million).

Extensive federal funding for scientific research can be problematic because ostensibly objective science is often tainted by political considerations. Funding may depend greatly upon the political opinions of the current majority in Congress and of the President. As a result, the sciences themselves can suffer. If projects are dependent on the stream of federal funding, then progress in some areas will be unavoidably staggered and limited.

Such is the fear for alternative energy research. The pushback against DoE loan programs, coupled with the redistribution of funds towards nuclear and fossil fuel divisions, may be taking away essential funds from the arena of alternative energy, an area that has not been economically competitive in the recent years but retains environmental importance. Political concerns, specifically the fear of being associated with the Solyndra scandal, may be the unstated reasoning behind this appropriations result, to the potential detriment of science.

SPENDING ON SELECTED AGENCIES, 1962 - 2012 (real)

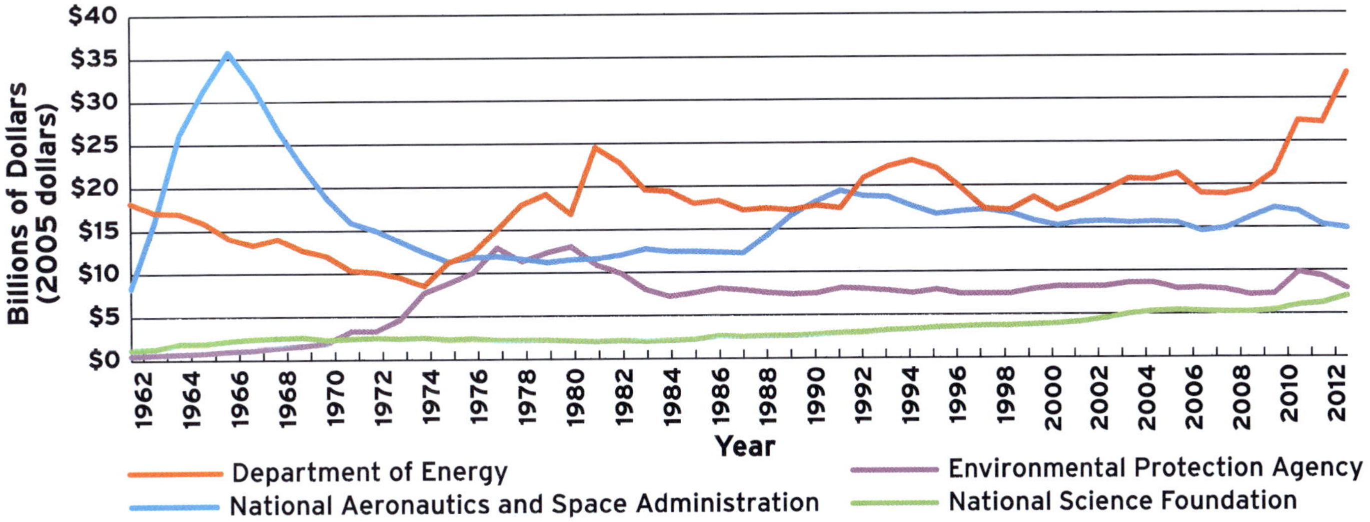

FIGURE 46 SOURCE: Budget of the U.S. Government FY 2013, http://www.gpo.gov/fdsys/pkg/BUDGET-2013-TAB/xls/BUDGET-2013-TAB-3-2.xls.

171 "FY2012 Budget: How Energy & Environment Fared," Sustainable Business, December 20, 2011, http://www.sustainablebusiness.com/index.cfm/go/news.display/id/23257.

NATURAL RESOURCES AND THE ENVIRONMENT

Environmental Protection Agency (EPA)

Jurisdiction: Enforces national standards through 13 offices, including the Office of Water and the Office of Emergency Response.

Current Funding: With large decreases expected, allocation of $8.4 billion for FY 2012 came as a pleasant surprise, only falling $524 million below the President's request and decreasing by $233 million from FY 2011.

History: Started in 1970, the EPA was created to use legal, written measures to protect human health and the environment.

Website: http://www.epa.gov/

Natural resources and the environment have struggled to secure funding since the start of the recession, and FY 2012 was no exception. The EPA is no stranger to suffering from a lack of funding in times of economic trouble, though. In fact, in FY 2011 the EPA faced serious cuts amounting to an 18.4 percent reduction in funds.[172]

National Oceanic and Atmospheric Administration (NOAA)

Jurisdiction: Serves mainly to explore environmental changes, such as climate and transportation. NOAA is part of the U.S. Department of Commerce.

Current Funding: The $5 billion awarded to the agency in FY 2012 did not meet the amount requested by the Obama administration, though it did constitute a 7 percent boost over FY 2011 levels.[173]

History: Created in 1970 to combine the work of the United States Coast Survey, United States Weather Bureau, and United States Commission of Fish and Fisheries.[174]

Website: http://www.noaa.gov/

NOAA's Joint Polar Satellite System (JPSS) project received a large part of the Administration's financial increase—$452 million. These funds will be used for the two civil polar weather satellites scheduled to launch in 2016.[175]

Following incidents like the Deepwater Horizon oil spill in the Gulf of Mexico in 2010, NOAA was also under increased pressure to provide funds for research into the cleanup and prevention of such tragedies. Most of the funds related to this on-going effort were actually obtained from BP, the oil company that operated the Deepwater Horizon rig, with the NOAA's Response and Restoration division expecting a total of $250 million from BP in order to restore, plan, implement, and monitor activities related to the spill.

172 "FY2012 Budget: How Energy & Environment Fared," Sustainable Business, December 20, 2011, http://www.sustainablebusiness.com/index.cfm/go/news.display/id/23257.
173 David Malakoff, "NOAA Environmental Satellites Win Funding," *Science Insider*, November 15, 2012, http://news.sciencemag.org/scienceinsider/2011/11/noaa-environmental-satellites.html.
174 "NOAA History: A Science Odyssey," NOAA, June 8, 2006, http://www.history.noaa.gov/welcome.html.
175 Dan Leone, "JPSS Contractor Foresees Adequate Funding for 2016 Launch," SpaceNews, December 2, 2011, http://spacenews.com/civil/111202-jpss-adequate-funding-2016-launch.html.

Summary

Funding for environmental and natural resources agencies, therefore, consisted of both cuts and increases in FY 2012. Several plans have fallen by the wayside, not receiving the funding or legislation required to enact them. The Obama administration's long-term goals of "continu[ing] to support greenhouse gas emissions reduction in the U.S." and the creation of the Climate Service are prime examples.[176] Other areas, like the Joint Polar Satellite System, felt renewed hope for survival after the disappointing financial setbacks of FY 2011.

HEALTH CARE AND RESEARCH

The most significant federal agency with a stake in health research is the National Institutes of Health. NIH is an agency of the U.S. Department of Health and Human Services, and it is the primary federal agency responsible for biomedical and health-related research.[177] Tracing its origins back to 1798 with the establishment of the Marine Hospital Service, NIH now awards more than 83 percent of its funding through almost 50,000 competitive grants to universities, medical schools, and other research institutions. In contrast to NSF, about 10 percent of the NIH budget supports projects conducted in its own laboratories.

Health research programs have maintained funding over the past few years, with NIH reaping the benefits of a 2009 stimulus package amendment allocating $10 billion of extra spending over two years to NIH. While the financial boost continued into FY 2012, the increase was modest, and NIH officials have pointed out indicators that suggest that such increases may not be enough. NIH overall received $30.7 billion, an increase of about 0.8 percent ($240 million). Such funds were directed towards one of NIH Director Francis Collins's top priorities: $576 million for the formation of the National Center for Advancing Translational Sciences, which would integrate fundamental therapeutic discoveries into the clinical environment.[178]

These humble increases mask a more telltale sign of funding problems for the NIH—only 18 percent of grant applications were approved in 2011, a record low. The NIH application success rate is often used as an indicator for how easily researchers are able to acquire money. NIH extramural research chief Sally Rockey noted that the decreased success is due not only to an increase in research grant proposals but also because a larger fraction of the money was devoted to grants that had already been awarded. (Most grants last from 3 to 5 years, and in 2011 a total of 78 percent of funds were already held by previous grant holders.) "This demonstrates how carefully we need to manage our funds since funding decisions in any one year have implications for the out years," said Rockey.[179]

In other words, grant awarders are forced to dole out grants without knowing whether allocations from Congress will remain stable. Give too many long-term grant promises without the appropriate funds, and programs are in trouble; refrain from distributing all available funds for a given year, and grant applicants who were turned away complain.

176 Amy Harder, "EPA Faces Third Straight Year of Cuts," *National Journal*, February 13, 2012, http://www.nationaljournal.com/2013-budget/epa-agency-faces-third-straight-year-of-cuts-20120213.
177 "About NIH," National Institutes of Health, http://www.nih.gov/about/index.html.
178 David Malakoff and Jocelyn Kaiser, "NIH, DOE Appear Headed For Small Budget Increases in 2012," *Science Insider*, December 15, 2011, http://news.sciencemag.org/scienceinsider/2011/12/nih-doe-appear-headed-for-small.html.
179 Jocelyn Kaiser, "NIH Examines What Drove Its Grant Success Rate to a Record Low," *Science Insider*, January 20, 2012, http://news.sciencemag.org/scienceinsider/2012/01/nih-examines-what-drove-its-grant.html.

NIH may have experienced increases for now, but officials are preparing for cutbacks in the years to come, with repercussions likely to affect grant applicants and various institutes of NIH alike.

SPENDING ON SELECTED RESEARCH PROGRAMS, FY 2012 (billions of dollars)

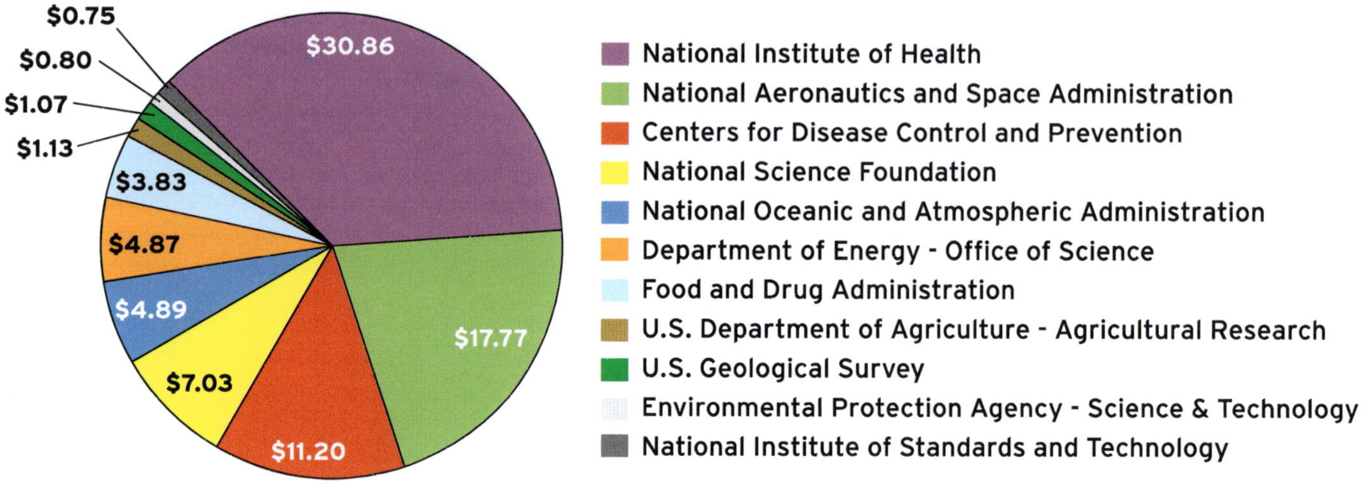

FIGURE 47 SOURCE: Science Insider, http://news.sciencemag.org/scienceinsider/budget_2013/.

A CAUTIOUS LOOK AHEAD

The overall scientific budget did not match the President's overarching plan to "double the budgets of three key science agencies" (DoE Office of Science, the NSF, and the National Institute of Standards and Technology), nor did it match the specific proposals made by the Obama administration and the agencies themselves. Indeed, the administration's proposals for FY 2012 stressed a push for increased funds, a movement that may have been rhetorical at its heart but was nonetheless significant as a sign of the nation's goals. While some areas were fortunate enough to share in this growth, like NIH and NSF, many other budget requests from the administration were clearly unrealistic in these times of economic trouble.

The Obama administration believed that innovation and continued investment in scientific and technological innovation would help America escape economic downturn, and the funding proposals for FY 2012 reflected that notion. However, allocated funding did not support this plan. Major budget reductions were abundant, and though there was some growth in the scientific and medical research budget, the motivations behind appropriations were not the same as they once were—research was no longer considered to be the economically profitable enterprise it once was, and new efforts were motivated by security concerns or reactions to disasters rather than by traditional reasons. The result, then, was a modest increase in the federal budget for scientific and medical research, accompanied by a restructuring of funds for many programs and agencies like NASA and the NSF.

★

OTHER CATEGORIES OF SPENDING: AGRICULTURAL SUBSIDIES

by Marina Bolotnikova

THE ORIGINS OF AGRICULTURAL SUBSIDIES

Though the federal government has been funding agriculture-related programs since the nineteenth century,[180] agricultural subsidies as we know them today originated with President Franklin D. Roosevelt's Agricultural Adjustment Act of 1933. The AAA authorized the federal government to pay farmers to leave a portion of their land uncultivated, reducing surplus and raising the market value of crops. Widely considered America's first farm bill, the AAA was introduced as a depression relief program for the more than one-quarter of Americans who were farmers during the Great Depression.[181]

THE PROBLEM OF AGRICULTURAL SUBSIDIES

Agricultural products receive subsidies because they do not behave well in the free market, according to Harwood Schaffer, an assistant professor at the University of Tennessee Agricultural Policy Analysis Center. They are subject to the irregularities of weather and disease, and the "true" market value of crops tends to vary with the irregularity of annual yields. Nor are crops price-responsive—consumer demand does not align neatly with the price or availability of agricultural products. In other words, people do not eat twice as much food if the price of food is halved.[182]

For these reasons, agricultural subsidies have remained a crucial component of federal spending. Lawmakers approve new farm bills approximately every five years that authorize spending not only on subsidies but also on other, agriculture-related programs. In fact, the majority of programs outlined in the Farm Bill are not strictly agricultural.[183] Fully two-thirds of funding authorized by the Bill is spent on nutritional programs. The most prominent of these is the Supplemental Nutrition Assistance Program (SNAP), formerly known as the Food Stamp Program, which was funded at over $85 billion in FY 2012.[184]

In contrast, agricultural spending makes up a relatively small proportion of spending authorized by the Farm Bill. In 2012, the federal government spent $19.2 billion on agricultural programs. About 62 percent of the total ($11.8 billion) was in mandatory spending. The majority of this spending on agriculture went to Farm Income Stabilization (FIS), the formal name for the agricultural subsidies program. Just over $1 billion in discretionary funding is also spent on FIS, putting federal spending on subsidies at a total of $12.6 billion, or about 66 percent of total spending on fully agriculture programs.

Other areas of agricultural spending include research and education. For example, the federal government funds research and education in sustainable agriculture through the Sustainable Agriculture Research and Education Program. In addition, the Foreign Agricultural Service, which develops foreign agricultural trade agreements and researches international agriculture, received $175 million in FY 2012, and federal inspection programs for

180 Daniel A. Sumner, "Farm Subsidy Tradition and Modern Agricultural Realities," University of California, Davis, May 15, 2007, www.aic.ucdavis.edu/research/farmbill07/aeibriefs/20070515_sumnerRationalesfinal.pdf.
181 "Agricultural Adjustment Act," Swarthmore College, http://www.sccs.swarthmore.edu/users/08/ajb/tmve/wiki100k/docs/Agricultural_Adjustment_Act.html.
182 Harwood Schaffer, interview by author, June 11, 2012.
183 "Analytical Perspectives," Budget of the U.S. Government FY 2013, February 13, 2012, http://www.gpo.gov/fdsys/pkg/BUDGET-2013-PER/pdf/BUDGET-2013-PER.pdf.
184 Julie Siple, "Proposed Food Stamp Cuts Could Push Minnesotans off the Program," Minnesota Public Radio, July 13, 2012, http://minnesota.publicradio.org/display/web/2012/07/13/news/food-stamp-proposal/; "U.S. Farm Bill: Frequently Asked Questions," SNAP to Health, http://www.snaptohealth.org/farm-bill-usda/u-s-farm-bill-faq/.

animal and crop facilities were funded at about $858 million.[185] Such miscellaneous programs, along with FIS, make up the federal government's more than $19 billion allocated to agricultural spending in FY 2012.

THE SUBSIDIES

Most FIS dollars are spent not on direct payments to farmers but on crop insurance. The most common form of insurance is revenue insurance, which guarantees farmers a yield and price. "If the revenue of crops is less than the expected revenue, the taxpayer pays the difference," explained Barry Goodwin, professor of agricultural and resource economics at North Carolina State University.[186] Most of this money subsidizes a few major crops: corn, soybeans, wheat, rice, and cotton (see Figure 48).[187]

Goodwin noted that the process by which crops are allocated subsidies is enormously complicated, but, in general, "it has a lot to do with which crops have the most political power," he said.[188]

Schaffer added that "part of it is a historical issue. When farm programs started, they dealt with major crops that affected the bulk of agricultural production." This model has remained largely unaltered over the past eighty years.[189]

AGRICULTURAL SUBSIDIES BY CROP (billions of dollars)

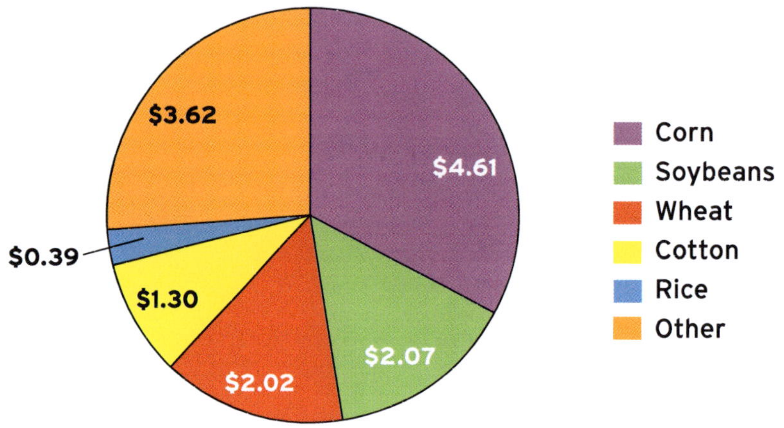

FIGURE 48

It is notable that the majority of crop subsidies are distributed to a small number of farms, due to the large degree of agricultural consolidation that took place in America during the twentieth century. Today, a small number of large farms produce the majority of crops grown in the U.S., which is reflected by the disproportionate subsidy dollars that they receive: about 10 percent of American farms receive 75 percent of subsidies.[190]

185 "Analytical Perspectives," Budget of the U.S. Government FY 2013, February 13, 2012, http://www.gpo.gov/fdsys/pkg/BUDGET-2013-PER/pdf/BUDGET-2013-PER.pdf.
186 Barry Goodwin, interview by author, June 6, 2012.
187 "The United States Summary Information," Environmental Working Group, www.farm.ewg.org/region.php?fips=00000&progcode=total&yr=2011.
188 Barry Goodwin, interview by author, June 6, 2012.
189 Harwood Schaffer, interview by author, June 11, 2012.
190 Barry Goodwin, interview by author, June 6, 2012.

THE CONTROVERSY

Agricultural subsidies have long been the subject of criticism from experts and policymakers. In recent years, subsidies have come under fire for their economic and health effects. Some experts argue that current subsidies prioritize the wrong crops, make unhealthy foods affordable, and benefit farmers who are already wealthy. "Payments go out regardless of need and to people who don't actually farm," according to the Environmental Working Group (EWG). "Sixty-two percent of farms in the United States do not collect any subsidy payments," EWG continued, in reference to the fact that the majority of subsidies benefit highly profitable business, not family farms.[191]

Some experts also argue that subsidies artificially lower the prices of unhealthy foods, such as high-fructose corn syrup and soy-based junk foods. But Goodwin countered that "subsidies just don't affect the price of our food that much. The links are hard to make."[192]

Acknowledging this point, EWG argued that "most economists agree that farm subsidies don't have much effect on food prices, but that misses the point. Instead of subsidizing raw materials for processed food," wrote EWG, "we should be using that money to improve access to healthy food. . . Even a tiny cut to [the five major crops] would dramatically increase funding for much healthier crops."[193]

Still others criticize subsidies on economic grounds. Schaffer argued that "we have a program that subsidizes not only farmers, but their insurance companies," which, he continued, is not an appropriate role for the federal government. Moreover, "farm programs shouldn't exist to ensure that farmers make profits," said Schaffer.

In summary, while some argue that subsidizing staple crops is crucial to protecting farms and protecting the U.S. from dependency on foreign food suppliers, others counter that subsidies do not make economic sense.[194]

THE FUTURE OF AGRICULTURAL SUBSIDIES

The new Farm Bill, scheduled to be approved in 2013, is likely to eliminate direct payments to farm landowners, which means that crop insurance subsidies will become the primary mechanism by which the federal government financially supports agriculture. This cut is expected to save the federal government $23 billion throughout the next ten years and is lauded by many progressive policymakers.[195]

Others, however, remain frustrated that the new bill reflects unchanged priorities. EWG, for example, wrote that "real reform would be to take all of the savings from ending direct payments and invest in programs that protect the environment and improve access to healthy food."[196]

191 Environmental Working Group, e-mail message to author, June 12, 2012.
192 Barry Goodwin, interview by author, June 6, 2012.
193 Environmental Working Group, e-mail message to author, June 12, 2012.
194 Harwood Schaffer, interview by author, June 11, 2012.
195 Cookson Beecher, "2012 Farm Bill Advances Under Pressure Over Healthy Food," Food Safety News, June 18, 2012, www.foodsafetynews.com/2012/06/if-the-usda-wants-us/.
196 Environmental Working Group, e-mail message to author, June 12, 2012.

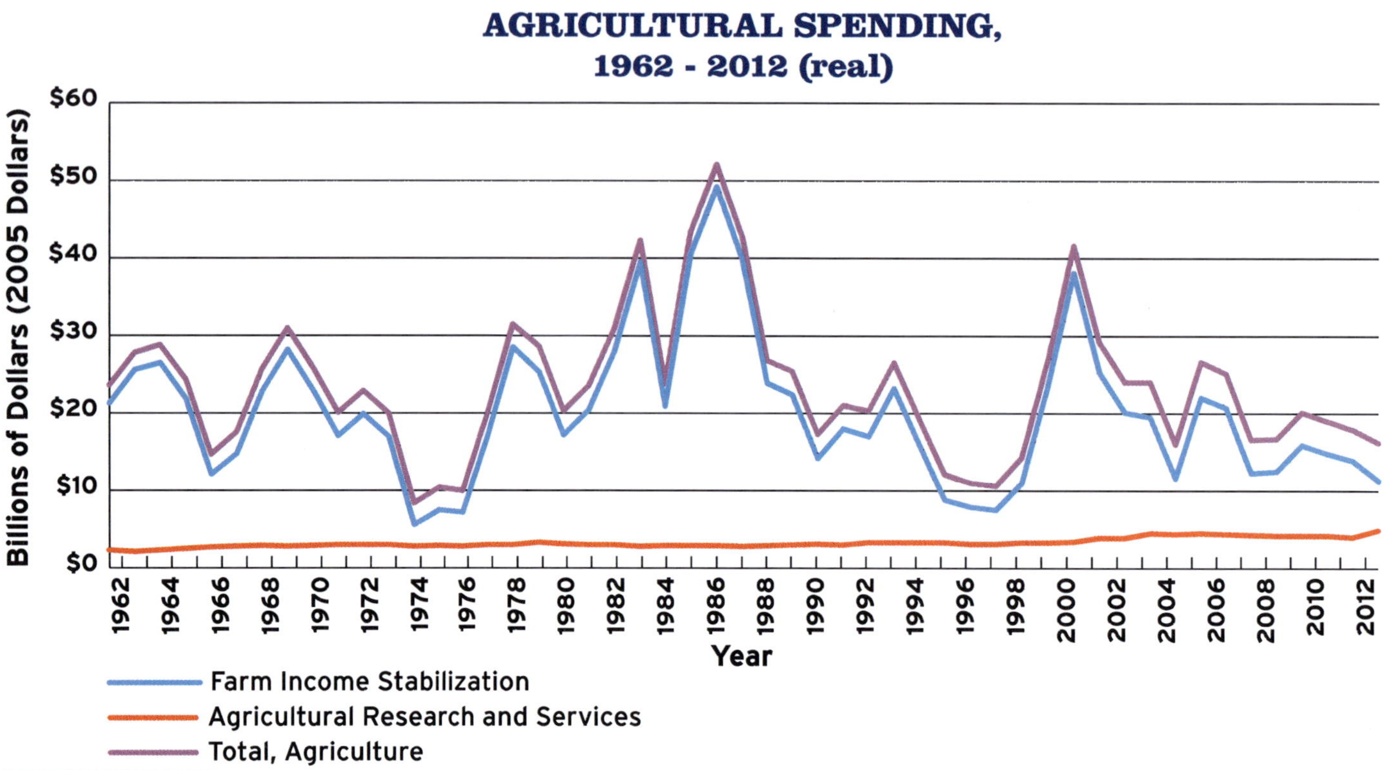

FIGURE 49

SOURCE: Budget of the U.S. Government FY 2013, http://www.gpo.gov/fdsys/pkg/BUDGET-2013-TAB/xls/BUDGET-2013-TAB-5-1.xls.

APPENDIX I: INDEX OF FIGURES AND TABLES

FIGURES

America's Finances

Recovering From the Recession

Entitlement Spending

APPENDIX I: INDEX OF FIGURES AND TABLES

National Defense & International Relations

Education, Science, & Technology

Other Categories of Spending

APPENDIX I: INDEX OF FIGURES AND TABLES

TABLES

America's Finances

Recovering From the Recession

Entitlement Spending

Foreign Relations & Defense

Education, Science, & Technology

★

ARUSA SPONSORS

American Education Foundation
http://www.americafound.org/

Institute of Politics at Harvard University
http://www.iop.harvard.edu/

Harvard Political Review
http://www.harvardpolitics.com/

U.S. FEDERAL GOVERNMENT

Congressional Budget Office
http://www.cbo.gov/

Government Accountability Office
http://www.gao.gov/

Joint Committee on Taxation
http://www.jct.gov/

Office of Management and Budget
http://www.whitehouse.gov/omb

President's Budget Requests ("Budget of the U.S. Government")
http://www.gpo.gov/fdsys/browse/collectionGPO.action?collectionCode=BUDGET

INDEPENDENT RESEARCH ORGANIZATIONS

Center on Budget and Policy Priorities
http://www.cbpp.org/

The Hamilton Project (Brookings Institution)
http://www.hamiltonproject.org/

Tax Policy Center (Brookings Institution and Urban Institute)
http://www.taxpolicycenter.org/

Printed in Dunstable, United Kingdom

91218899R00063